Illustrated
True Crime

Illustrated True Crime

Edited by Colin Wilson and Damon Wilson

Magpie Books, London

Constable & Robinson Ltd
3 The Lanchesters
162 Fulham Palace Road
London W6 9ER

First published 2002 by Robinson, an imprint of Constable & Robinson Ltd,
as *The Mammoth Book of Illustrated Crime*

This edition published by Magpie Books,
an imprint of Constable & Robinson Ltd 2005
www.constablerobinson.com

ISBN 1 84529 271 5

Produced in association with Getty Images
Printed and bound in China

3 5 7 9 10 8 6 4

Contents

INTRODUCTION: A BRIEF HISTORY OF MODERN CRIME

The 20th century will be seen by future historians as the beginning of a new and frighteningly ugly chapter in the history of crime.

To trace this era of violence and brutality to its roots, we have to start with the aftermath of the American Civil War (1861–65), when dozens of army veterans, like Jesse James and his brother Frank, decided that a return to the old hardworking life of the farm or the small town was too boring to contemplate, and decided to live the life of outlaws. It must have seemed to them that in this great new age of railroads and steamboats, it was a pity to waste your life working as a cowboy or farmhand for a few dollars a week. What happened, of course, is that many of these outlaws came to an early and violent end, or spent most of their lives in prison. Jesse James, Billy the Kid, Butch Cassidy and the Sundance Kid, the Dalton brothers, all came to feel nostalgic about the peaceful life of the farm they had abandoned – like their gangster descendants of the 1930s, Dillinger, Bonnie and Clyde and Baby Face Nelson.

Meanwhile, on the other side of the Atlantic, a mysterious maniac known as Jack the Ripper was also inaugurating a new era in the history of crime. The five Ripper murders of 1888 are a watershed. They are still unsolved, although most modern "ripperologists" will agree that a highly likely candidate is the cotton merchant James Maybrick, an arsenic addict who developed a psychotic hatred of "whores" out of jealousy caused by his unfaithful wife Florence, and may have committed the mutilation murders of prostitutes as a kind of twisted revenge on women in general – a curious kind of logic that, as we shall see, is typical of the "serial killer". The Ripper murders are significant for another reason: they may be conveniently regarded as the starting point of the "Age of Sex Crime". In the 18th and 19th centuries, most of the "criminal classes" were too poor to commit murder for anything as unprofitable as rape: sex was so cheap that even a virgin could be had for five shillings in mid-19th century London. The result is that there are few sex crimes in the police records of the early and mid-19th century. The contemporaries of Jack the Ripper did not even recognize them as sex crimes; one favourite theory was that the Ripper was a "religious maniac" who wanted to reduce the number of "fallen women" in London.

In France in the mid-1890s, the "French Ripper" Joseph Vacher, a mentally subnormal vagrant, carried out a series of sex-mutilation attacks on boys, girls and older women (eleven in all) and was caught only by chance. He was executed in 1897. Meanwhile, the political scandal of the Dreyfus case – in which a corrupt administration allowed a Jewish army officer to pay the penalty for a crime he did not commit – seemed to support the contention of the anarchists, that all power corrupts. Eighty years later, in the final decades of the 20th century, "Red Brigades" in Italy, Germany and Japan would attempt to establish a new social order by killing and kidnapping the kind of "corrupt" politicians they thought responsible.

Meanwhile, still in France, a young police clerk named Alphonse Bertillon had been giving much thought to the problem of a simple identification system which would allow the police to check on a newly arrested suspect and find out whether he had a criminal record. Photography was notoriously unreliable because the time it took to expose a photographic plate was too long to take a good picture of a struggling prisoner. About 1880, Bertillon devised a system of 11 measurements – circumference of the head, length of forearm, middle and ring fingers – which would quickly identify a suspect who had been measured before, and anthropometry or "Bertillonage" became one the first effective methods of scientific crime-fighting. By the time of the Jack the Ripper murders, Bertillon had founded a new Department of Judicial Identity at the Surete, the first in the world.

Alas, his triumph was short-lived. By 1891, an English scientist, Sir Francis Galton, cousin of Charles Darwin, was studying fingerprints, and in 1892 he published a book on their classification. In 1902 fingerprinting was adopted by Scotland Yard. It was much simpler than the Bertillon method, for although the latter included fingerprinting, the card with the criminal's description was not classified by fingerprints. So a case in which a fingerprint had been found at the scene of the crime might involve searching thousands of cards. For more than a decade, Bertillon stubbornly refused to see the importance of giving precedence to fingerprints, to the detriment of French crime detection, a situation that continued until he retired, when the British system was promptly adopted.

Meanwhile, in Russia, political violence was becoming an everyday occurrence. The Communism of Karl Marx and the Anarchism of Prince Kropotkin had inspired a new generation of social revolutionaries, who believed that the answer to social injustice lay in new explosives like nitro-glycerine, dynamite and gelignite. On 1 March 1871, the relatively liberal Tsar Alexander II was killed by a bomb made of nitro-glycerine enclosed in thick glass. The result was counterproductive; the next Tsar, Alexander III, went in for a policy of savage repression, implemented by his police chief Plehve, who became the most hated man in Russia. In July 1904, in the reign of Nicholas II, someone tossed a bomb under Plehve's carriage, and it took three days to gather up the pieces. The result: more repression, which included the massacre by Cossacks of hundreds of peaceful marchers in St Petersburg on 22 January 1905. (The Tsar enquired anxiously "Are you sure they've killed enough people?") The result was uprisings all over Russia, all repressed with the same savagery. Nicholas II had virtually guaranteed his own eventual murder.

The Tsar temporarily established peace by agreeing to an elected people's parliament called the Duma. The problem was that, like England's pig-headed King

Charles I, he was convinced that God had appointed him absolute monarch, and kept on thwarting the designs of the Duma until, in a fit of pique, he closed it down.

The man who might have ended social revolution in Russia was a remarkable progressive conservative named Peter Stolypin, whose courage and commonsense could have reconciled the Tsar and the Duma. But the revolutionaries failed to recognize that he was basically an ally, and made several attempts to assassinate him, in one of which his house was blown up and his daughter crippled for life. But the Tsar was distrustful of his new Prime Minister, and failed to provide him with adequate protection when he and Stolypin attended an opera in Kiev in 1911, and Stolypin was shot down by a revolutionary named Bogrov.

Three years later, Russia would be drawn into the First World War after the assassination of Archduke Franz Ferdinand at Sarajevo. Defeats brought social unrest, and the Tsar was deposed by the 1917 Revolution. He and his family would die in a cellar in Ekaterinburg on 16 July 1918. No one who has studied the history of Russia under Nicholas II can avoid feeling that he deserved his fate.

It was during the First World War that spying properly developed. Espionage had been around during the American Civil War, but at a level that strikes us as almost amateurish. The development of radio and encoding machines now changed the face of war. The British had an extraordinary piece of luck when the German codebooks were found clutched in the arms of a corpse dragged out of the icy waters of the Baltic. The Russians handed them over to Winston Churchill, and the foundations of German naval defeat were laid. The 20th century had taken one more step towards making war more efficient and ruthless.

The new spirit of brutality is typified in a story about the theft of a German military code. The British spymaster, Admiral "Blinker" Hall, learned that the radio engineer who was transmitting coded messages from Brussels was an Austro-Hungarian named Alexander Szek, who was born in Croydon, south London.

Szek's family was persuaded to write him a letter begging him to work for the British, and it was smuggled to him by a British agent. Szek agreed to steal the German code little by little – he worked with a German Intelligence officer who dictated to him. But Szek was too timid to be a good spy, and insisted that he should be smuggled to England as soon as the copying was complete. His "handler" pointed out that in that case, all their effort would have been wasted, since the Germans would change the code as soon as he vanished. Still Szek insisted. Then, when the code was complete, Szek was found dead in his lodgings. His family was told that he had been killed by the Germans or by a burglar; but the truth, almost certainly, is that he was killed by the British, who probably justified their treachery by arguing that his death would save thousands of British lives.

The victory of Britain and France – due largely to American intervention – in the First World War brought chaos to Europe, particularly to the losers, and the huge reparations demanded by Allies sent Germany into bankruptcy, and created the ideal conditions for the rise of Hitler and the Nazis. Hitler was driven fundamentally by hatred of the Jews and communists, whom he believed to be responsible for everything rotten and decadent in the modern world. His answer, as we now know, was mass extermination. It is almost impossible for us to understand how any sane human being could believe that the murder of millions of his fellows could be regarded as a justifiable means to an end, but this brutal morality is somehow typical of the 20th century. In retrospect, the rise of Nazism can be recognized as one of the greatest disasters in human history.

As with so many criminals, Hitler brought about his own downfall. Determined to break the pact he had made with Stalin, he planned Operation Barbarossa, the invasion of the Soviet Union. But he went into a wild rage with the Serbs for reneging on an agreement, and ordered the Luftwaffe to destroy Belgrade. It took a month, and the delay cost Hitler the war, for he invaded Russia in June 1941 instead of May, and was caught by the Russian winter when his forces were in sight of Moscow. The Russian armies made a tremendous counter-attack in December 1941, and the war was lost. Lord Acton's dictum that power corrupts should also be taken to mean that it destroys all judgement and common sense. One result of the Moscow setback was that Hitler took personal control of the war, and made so many wrong-headed decisions that he ensured the Nazi defeat. The suicide of Hitler allowed another paranoid criminal to escape the fate he deserved. Joseph Stalin had been murdering political colleagues since he became leader of the Party in 1927. During the 1930s his "purges" cost the lives of so many of his most intelligent colleagues and best generals that it would almost cost him the war. He was saved only by a Japanese decision – relayed by Russian spies – not to invade Russia from the east, so that Stalin was enabled to move thousands of troops from the Pacific coast just in time, and turn back the German advance on Moscow. It seems possible that Stalin died – in 1953 – as a result of poisoning by his own doctors.

The end of the First World War caused America to take one of the most disastrous steps in its history. Always prone to Puritanism and outbursts of morality, America took the fatal plunge into Prohibition in 1919, guaranteeing that for the remainder of the century, the country would be dominated by gangsters. The demand for bootleg liquor brought Al Capone from New York to Chicago, and soon rival gangs were murdering one another at a rate that convinced ordinary citizens that they would soon be rid of these predators. In fact, all that happened was that the law of survival of the fittest ensured the development of a new breed of criminal who was as ruthless as his political counterparts. The St Valentine's Day Massacre (14 February 1929) showed that Capone was willing to kill as many of his rivals as was necessary to ensure his own total control. Two hundred and twenty-seven Capone rivals or challengers were murdered in the 1920s.

The St Valentine's Day Massacre was Capone's major mistake. Citizens all over America were outraged, and orders came from President Hoover that Capone was to be jailed, no matter how. He could not be indicted for murder, but an intelligent treasury official named Elmer L. Irey had the inspired notion of indicting him for non-payment of income tax. With the help of Capone's business agent, Eddie O'Hare, Federal agents obtained some Capone account books that proved that his income ran to millions of dollars, on which tax had never been paid. Capone was sentenced to 11 years.

When Prohibition was repealed under Franklin Roosevelt in 1933, everyone hoped that this was the end of the mobs. Gangsters like Lucky Luciano, Albert Anastasia, Joe Adonis and Frank Costello were afraid this might be the case, and came up with their own answer: a national crime syndicate whose income would be derived from drugs, brothels and gaming. The law enforcement arm of this syndicate became known as Murder Incorporated, and until 1940, its existence was unsuspected by the police. Then a gangster named Abe Reles (known as Kid Twist) was betrayed by a fellow gangster, and accused of a murder that had occurred in 1933. Faced with the certainty of the electric chair, Reles decided to "sing", and for the first time, the activities of Murder Incorporated were described. Half a dozen killers went to the electric chair before, on 12 November 1941, Reles fell to his death from the sixth floor window of his hotel on Coney Island – with seven police guards apparently looking the other way. His death remains a mystery.

Lucky Luciano had been in jail since 1935. It was Luciano who had ordered the killing of a New York racketeer named Dutch Schultz, after Schultz had decided to murder District Attorney Thomas E. Dewey. The Syndicate, led by Luciano, was alarmed, knowing that the murder of a D.A. would bring a crackdown. When Schultz ignored the order to forget it, he was assassinated in a New Jersey eating house. Unfortunately for Luciano, the murder rebounded on him. As he died in hospital, Schultz croaked that "the boss himself" was responsible for this. Luciano was arrested on charges of extortion, and was sentenced to 30 to 50 years in prison. Again, it looked as if the forces of law had triumphed. Then, in 1942, the French liner Normandie was burned down to the waterline in the Hudson River – obviously an act of wartime sabotage. The waterfront was still controlled by Luciano, even from prison, and Naval Intelligence decided to ask for Luciano's help. In exchange for agreeing that Luciano would be paroled at the end of the war, and transferred immediately to a more comfortable prison, the Syndicate – represented by Meyer Lansky – agreed to keep the waterfront free of sabotage, and lived up to its promise.

When the Americans invaded Italy, a message from Luciano to the "godfather" of Sicily ensured that the American forces received full cooperation. Mussolini had crushed the Mafia; now the Americans resuscitated it. And although Luciano was deported in 1946, he was able to call together all the godfathers of Murder Incorporated in Havana, Cuba, and although Luciano was quickly ordered out of Cuba by the American-backed Batista government, he continued to run his rackets from Naples, where he died of a heart attack in 1962.

Perhaps, if anyone should read this book in 2100, they will be able to look back comfortably on the bad old days when America was in the grip of racketeers. But at the time of writing the bad old days are still with us ...

For the historian of crime, the most ominous development in the 20th century was the rise of sex crime. As already noted, sex crime (in our modern sense of the word) hardly existed until the late 19th century. We can see why sex crime was so long in arriving. In the 19th century, life was hard for 99 percent of the population, and exhausted men and women fell asleep at the end of a 16-hour day. Only the wealthy one percent had time to treat sex as a diversion, and for a sex-driven male there were plenty of pretty dairymaids. (That remarkable anonymous document *My Secret Life*, published in the late 19th century, shows that a wealthy man could have had practically any woman he wanted, from the wives of friends to ten-year-old girls.)

The first sign of a major change of attitude towards sex occurs sometime before 1820, with the rise of the pornography industry. The pornography of earlier ages had been largely anti-clerical, consisting of the confessions of lubricious monks or nymphomaniac nuns. Early 19th century pornography sets out to create an atmosphere of feverish sensuality based on a feeling of "the forbidden": schoolgirls are seduced by the schoolmasters, upper-class young girls spy on the butler masturbating, and get so excited they allow him to take their virginity. The premise is that sex is infinitely "naughty" and infinitely delightful.

I suspect that one of the major changes in the male's attitude to sex was the invention of the typewriter in 1867, and the fact that relatively poor young ladies could now support themselves as typists. As the new class of working girls increased, a whole new type of "forbidden woman" came into existence, like the vestal virgins in ancient Rome. When James Boswell walked down Piccadilly or the Haymarket in 1750, he knew he could secure virtually any pretty girl, but if Boswell had walked through central London in 1890, he would have been surrounded by prim young ladies who would have been outraged if he had tried to pick them up.

So the predatory male began to daydream of rape – the rape of prim, respectable girls. In 1895, the case of Theodore Durrant, a San Francisco Sunday school teacher, achieved worldwide newspaper coverage; he lured young ladies into the vestry of the Baptist church, excused himself for a moment, then reappeared naked and throttled the girl into submission. One victim was found in the library, the other in the belfry. A third had screamed and fled. Durrant, who was hanged in 1898, was one of the first of a new type of criminal that would become commonplace in the 20th century: the male who thought it was worth killing for sex. What is so significant about the Durrant case is that he must have known that he could not get away with it, and that he would probably pay with his life. He would have had no trouble finding prostitutes in San Francisco in 1895. But this frustrated young man, surrounded by Victorian prudery, gazed at these demure young ladies in their long dresses, and felt that life would not be worth living unless he was allowed to find out what they looked like without their clothes. Oddly enough, the future change from ankle-length dresses to miniskirts and bikinis made no difference. Seventy years later, in a far more permissive age, another Theodore, Theodore Bundy, felt exactly the same and devoted his life to rape.

So the age of sex crime began. It got off to a slow start. There are no significant sex crimes in the decade between 1900 and the First World War. In effect, society was still governed by Victorian morality. But in 1913, a Hungarian named Bela Kiss began a brief career of mass murder when he advertised for ladies needing a husband, and received dozens of replies. Kiss was well known in the brothels of Budapest, where he was regarded as virtually insatiable. But the prime motive had not been sex but money; like the French "bluebeard" Landru (who also began operating at about this time), he decided that middle-aged women were easy prey. When Kiss went off to the war in 1914, he left seven sealed drums in his workshop – they proved to contain the corpses of seven naked women. Kiss was never caught, or even seen again. As to whether Kiss should be classified as a sex criminal, it is worth noting that the money he made was promptly spent in Budapest's brothels. Like Landru, he was an obsessive seducer; seduction for both men was a psychological as well as a physical necessity. Landru was an unsuccessful petty crook who had spent much time in jail before he embarked on his career as a lady killer, and his talent for seduction provided him with balm for his damaged ego. And this theme runs throughout the history of sex crime in the 20th century.

Nevertheless, perhaps the most typical herald of the future was not a sex crime, but the 1924 murder of schoolboy Bobbie Franks by two University of Chicago students, Nathan Leopold and Richard Loeb, both from relatively affluent families. They had no clear motive except to prove to each other (they were lovers) that they were not the slaves of a narrow social morality. Their original plan, to kidnap a girl and rape her, was dropped in favour of kidnapping a friend of Loeb's younger brother, and demanding ransom. The scheme failed because Leopold, the more sensitive and intelligent of the two (and the least dominant) dropped his glasses near the body, and because they were of unusual design, they were traced to him. And although he claimed he had lost them when bird watching, contradictions in the testimony of the two young men soon convinced the investigators of their guilt, and under interrogation, they confessed. In spite of a clamour for their execution, both were sentenced to life imprisonment.

The case represents a watershed in the history of crime because it was apparently motiveless. It was not committed for money or revenge or sex, but simply for "kicks". Of course, tyrants throughout history have killed for the same reason. And in 1912, in a novel called *The Vatican Cellars*, the French novelist Andre Gide had invented a character called Lafcadio who pushes a stranger off a train as a "gratuitous act". Leopold and Loeb put Gide's fantasy into practise, and the age of the "motiveless crime" had arrived.

As to "lustmord" (as the Germans call sexual murder), there is a sense in which Peter Kurten, the "Dusseldorf sadist", is the archetypal sex killer of the 20th century. From childhood on, Kurten was totally obsessed by sex – with animals as well as women. And it was when having intercourse with a sheep, and stabbing it at the same time, that he discovered that violence could intensify his sexual urge. (The serial killer Henry Lee Lucas would later make the same discovery.) During years spent in prison, often in solitary confinement, he spent his time in sexual fantasy, which became steadily more violent as his physical urges flagged. In 1925 he returned to Düsseldorf and was delighted with a blood-red sunset. Then began his reign of terror. He began with arson, and widely spaced sexual attacks, but by 1929, was attacking his victims with a hammer, knife, scissors or strangulation, simply because violence and the sight of blood brought him to a sexual climax.

Kurten makes us aware of a kind of "law of diminishing returns" in sexual violence. Like Theodore Durrant, most sex criminals begin with a desire to commit straightforward rape, motivated by the kind of fevered curiosity that drives Peeping Toms. The victim is raped, and possibly killed to prevent recognition. Then, as the rapes progress, the sex becomes increasingly sadistic, and inflicting pain and indignity becomes an essential part of the excitement. Ted Bundy admitted that the things he had done to his last victim, a 12-year-old schoolgirl named Kim Leach, were so horrific that he was ashamed to describe them.

There appears to be some kind of psychological law that sex crime always develops in the direction of sadism. The First World War seemed to release a flood of sexual violence. This, of course, had something to do with the "sexual liberation" of the 1920s, for as the disruption of the Victorian world carried away the old inhibitions, rape inevitably became more common. In retrospect, it looks almost as if society was permeated by a kind of telepathic sexuality that affected everyone like a germ. Among its victims between 1920 and 1940 were Earle Nelson, Albert Fish, Carl Panzram and the sadist who committed the unsolved "Cleveland Torso" murders. All these cases deserve a brief description.

Between 1926 and late 1927, a man who became known as "the Gorilla Murderer" wandered across America, then into Canada, knocking on doors of houses with a "Room to Let" sign and, if the landlady was alone, strangling and raping her repeatedly. Earle Nelson had committed 22 murders before he was caught in Canada, where he was hanged in January 1928. It is worth noting that Nelson had suffered a severe head injury as a child, and that this is a feature found in many sex killers. No one had ever before committed sex murder on this scale.

Albert Fish, a mild-looking old man, was arrested in New York in December 1934 for the murder of 10-year-old Grace Budd; her family had been so convinced of his harmlessness that they allowed him to take her to a "birthday party", from which she never returned. Six years after her disappearance he wrote her parents a letter admitting to having killed and eaten her. Brilliant detective work tracked down the letter writer, who proved to be a 64-year-old painter and decorator who had been practising sexual perversions – like driving needles into his genitals – for years. Frederick Wertham, the psychiatrist who examined him, wrote: "He felt driven to torment and kill children", and said that Fish had more sexual perversions than any criminal he had encountered. Fish had been killing children for decades, and may have killed dozens. He was a sadist and masochist, and when told he would be electrocuted, remarked with unconscious humour: "It will be the great thrill of my life."

Carl Panzram is one of the most typical sex killers of the century. Arrested in 1928, this bear-like man with a limp declared that the charge of stealing a radio was a joke. Asked why, he replied: "Because I've killed too many people to worry about a charge like that." No one believed him. But in prison in Washington D.C., a young guard named Henry Lesser became friendly with Panzram after he had been beaten up by prison guards, and Lesser had sent him a dollar by a "trusty". When he realized this was a genuine gesture of sympathy, Panzram's eyes filled with tears, and he said that if Lesser could get him some writing materials, he would write his autobiography. The result was a book that was a horrifying catalogue of crime, including dozens of homosexual rapes and motiveless murders. Panzram was full of a frenzied resentment against the world and hatred of society. The key to Panzram was an enormous dominance that meant he would never give way under punishment. He would smash up his cell and be beaten unconscious by the guards, or be hung by the wrists for days; yet when he was released, his first response would be to throw his food in the guard's face. Punishment had turned him into a violent mass of hatred. But this led him to a strange logic. "If I couldn't injure those who had injured me, then I would injure someone else." Predictably, the murders he committed only plunged him deeper and deeper into self-contempt.

Now this strange logic deserves a word to itself. Jean Paul Sartre called it "magical thinking", by which he meant a form of unrealistic behaviour that simply fails to achieve its objective, like an ostrich burying its head in the sand. Sartre gives an example of a girl who faints when about to be attacked – trying to make a problem go away by refusing to face it. "Magical thinking" is epitomized by a joke about an Arab who returns to his family with an umbrella, explaining: "It is an English invention – if you want it to rain you leave it at home". This peculiar form of non-logic seems typical of criminals, who are adept at blaming other people for problems that are actually their own fault. It can be seen, for example, in the activities of the Italian Red Brigade of the 1970s, attempting to bring about an ideal society by murdering "capitalist pigs" at random. The problem with such logic is simply that it fails to achieve its objective. It is an expression of emotion rather than reason.

Panzram's "magical thinking" led to a self-hatred that resulted in what amounted to suicide. Before the murders had started, a liberal prison governor named Murphy, aware of Panzram's reputation for being uncontrollable, had offered to let him walk out of the prison if he would promise to return by nightfall. Panzram accepted, with no intention of keeping his promise; yet something made him go back when the time came. He did this many times, and was allowed increasing freedom, until one day he got drunk and failed to return. Captured after a gun battle, he was unable to look Murphy in the face. This episode seems to have been a turning point; his hatred of society became self-hatred, and he went on to commit 20 murders in this state of mind. He finally killed a prison overseer and was sentenced to death. He refused all offers from supporters like H.L. Mencken – to whom Lesser had sent the book – to try to get him reprieved, and on the scaffold in September 1930 told the hangman: "Hurry it up, you hoosier bastard. I could hang a dozen men while you're fooling around."

The Cleveland Torso killer could be regarded as America's equivalent of Jack the Ripper. Also known as "the Mad Butcher" and "the head hunter" (because he liked to decapitate victims), he preyed on vagrants, and dumped their mutilated bodies in an overgrown railway cutting called Kingsbury Run – sometimes two bodies at a time. Between 1935 and 1938, the Mad Butcher killed 12 men and women; then the murders ceased. What little we know about the killer has to be inferred. He must have had a place of his own – not just a room but a house, since the time-consuming mutilations must have been committed by someone who was not afraid of being interrupted. And he must have possessed a car, to transport the bodies to Kingsbury Run. This argues that he was a comparatively rich man, suffering from some severe psychosis.

It has even been suggested that the Mad Butcher may have been responsible for another horrific murder that happened in the 1940s in Los Angeles: the unsolved Black Dahlia case. In January 1947, the body of Elizabeth Short, a would-be film actress, was found on waste ground; she had been hung upside down, tortured with a knife and then cut in half at the waist – forensic evidence indicated that this had all happened while she was still alive. The case caused the same widespread shock as the Jack the Ripper murders of half a century earlier, and the police received dozens of false confessions. This in itself raises a question of deep psychological interest: why should so many men confess to the crime? The implication is that they all wished they had committed it, and that Elizabeth Short's killer was some kind of enviable celebrity. This again tells us something about our society: a society so complex and demanding that it creates in many individuals a sense of loss of identity, of being a nonentity. Such alienated individuals daydream of fame, and even a sadistic killer seems an exciting role model. What we are talking about here is not sexual obsession so much as a strange variant of the craving for self-esteem that all human beings experience. Panzram's autobiography makes it clear that he became a mass murderer because of a total collapse of self-esteem. His betrayal of the trust of Warden Murphy had led to a sense of worthlessness; he remarked to Lesser: "What gets me is how the heck any man of your intelligence ... can still be friendly to a thing like me, when I even despise and detest my own self." He killed as a gesture of self-disgust, as he might have wallowed in mud.

The self-esteem motivation plays an increasing role in murder in the second half of the 20th century. In 1959, a jazz musician named Melvin Rees committed a number of sex murders on the east coast of the United States, including a family of four – he killed the father and baby in order to be able to kidnap and rape the wife and five-year-old daughter. Rees had told a friend: "You can't say it's wrong to kill – only individual standards make it right or wrong." The friend reported his suspicions to the police, who discovered in Rees's home the gun with which the family had been shot. Rees, a mild, quietly-spoken, intelligent man, was found guilty and executed in 1961.

Ian Brady, the Moors Murderer, was another intelligent and well-read man who shared Panzram's hatred of society and "dreamed of revenge". The five murders he and Myra Hindley committed between 1963 and 1965 were not sex crimes so much as crimes of self-esteem; Brady was shaking his fist at society. Myra Hindley even described how, after one of the murders, the atheist Brady shook his fist at the sky and shouted: "Take that, you bastard!"

This element of self-esteem again played a major role in the crimes of the Charles Manson "Family" in 1969. Manson felt that society had treated him badly

– in 1967, at the age of 33, he had spent more than half his life in jail. In the Haight-Ashbury district of San Francisco, he discovered that he had the charisma of a religious messiah, and soon became the guru of a group of hippies he called his "children". Like so many "messiahs" he became increasingly paranoid, and began to dream of causing a revolution by turning black against white – a project he called Helter Skelter. In July, a Manson disciple named Bobby Beausoleil stabbed to death a musician, Gary Hinman, on Manson's orders. Two weeks later, the "Family" entered the house of pregnant film star Sharon Tate, who was giving a dinner party for three guests. All four were murdered. Manson was not present on this occasion, but the following evening, he led six of his Family to the home of supermarket owner Leno LaBianca, and his wife Rosemary, and ordered his followers to kill them, intensifying the panic caused by the Tate murders. Two months later, the police arrested most of the Manson family for vandalising a bulldozer. In prison, Susan Atkins – one of the Tate killers – dropped hints about her involvement in the murders; under police questioning she soon told the whole story. At the trial, Manson tried to turn it into an indictment of modern society, arguing with typical "magical" logic that if the government had killed innocent civilians in Vietnam, he and his Family were somehow not guilty of murdering six people. But the jury disagreed, and Manson and three female disciples were convicted of murder and sentenced to death (later commuted to life imprisonment). Other members of the gang were later sentenced to long periods in jail. The prosecutor, Vincent Bugliosi, guessed that the Manson Family probably killed about 35 people.

And from 1960 on, it is cases of multiple murder that figure as the prominent crimes of each decade: in the 1960s, the Boston Strangler (Albert DeSalvo), the Moors case and Manson; in the 1970s, Ted Bundy, Dean Corll, John Gacy, the Hillside Stranglers (Buono and Bianchi), the Yorkshire Ripper; in the 1980s, Henry

Lee Lucas, Richard Ramirez ("the Night Stalker"), the Green River killer, Jeffrey Dahmer, Dennis Nilsen, Andrei Chikatilo, Leonard Lake; in the 90s, Fred West, Ivan Millat (the Austalian "backpacker killer"), Gerard Schaefer, Danny Rolling, and Anatoly Onoprienko, Russia's worst mass murderer since Andrei Chikatilo (who had killed 56 between 1978 and 1990).

The term "serial killer" was coined by FBI agent Robert Ressler some time in the early 1980s, to describe killers like Henry Lee Lucas, who claimed to have committed 360 murders (a total equalled by Pedro Lopez, "the monster of the Andes"). And as the decade progressed with killers like Richard Ramirez, Leonard Lake and Andrei Chikatilo, it became clear that this type of multiple murder was virtually a new phenomenon – that the serial killer murders almost casually, as a kind of habit.

I noted the cause of this problem in 1958, in a book called *The Age of Defeat*, and had quoted Alexis de Tocqueville's *Democracy in America* to the effect that the average American "is habitually engaged in the contemplation of a very puny object, namely himself, and that when he raises his looks higher, he then perceives nothing but the immense form of society at large, too big and impersonal to allow him any sense of belonging." In the days of the pioneers, all Americans had a sense of being unique individuals, like people in a village; in the modern world, the talented individual feels that he is negated by the sheer number of his fellow human beings. Most serial killers and many murderers (in the US and elsewhere) are driven by this sense of being nobodies. When an 18-year-old student named Robert Smith shot five women and two children in a beauty parlour in Mesa, Arizona in 1966, he told the police: "I wanted to get known, to get myself a name."

I would argue that the 20th century differed from earlier centuries in one peculiar respect: that it would be possible to write its history almost entirely in terms of its murderers. And this book attempts to show some of that history by way of photographs.

1 FROM GASLIGHT TO TOMMY GUN

The American Civil War was a brutal and basically pointless conflict, but, in retrospect, we can see that it brought modern America into existence: a society crackling with immense vitality and enterprise, in which anything could happen. Politicians had always been prone to corruption, but the post-1865 party bosses – like New York's Boss Tweed – went into politics primarily to make a fortune.

In the 1860s, the first Mafia appeared in Italy, after the unification of the Italian states under Garibaldi. The criminal brotherhoods of Sicily supported Garibaldi and so achieved a kind of respectability, and once the foreign invaders had been evicted, the Mafia settled down to the business of extortion and bribery with a sense of being untouchable.

At the turn of the century, Sicily's "godfather", Don Vito Cascio Ferro, is believed to have organized the importation of the Mafia into America, although a bandit named Esposito had already moved there in 1880. New Orleans, with its Italian population, was the natural choice, and the criminals set out to achieve political power.

In England, criminally speaking, the 19th century moved along more sedately, with a series of famous domestic murders – Dr Pritchard, Florence Bravo, Adelaide Bartlett – until Jack the Ripper burst on the scene in 1888 with an impact that we now find hard to understand. One old lady was so shocked as a newsboy yelled "Latest 'orrible murder in Whitechapel" that she dropped dead. Jack the Ripper would have been delighted. The one thing we know from the letters attributed to him (some of which are undoubtedly genuine) is that he was a paranoiac who was full of hatred for society.

In early 20th-century America, the crimes that attracted most attention continued to be basically "domestic" murders, like Harry Thaw's murder of the architect Stanford White, or Chester Gillette's drowning of his unwanted girlfriend Grace Brown (on which Theodore Dreiser based *An American Tragedy*).

In France, the Steinheil case (1908) and the Mme Caillaux case illustrated the French preoccupation with domestic scandal, while in Venice, the case of Marie Tarnovska, who left a trail of suicide and murder, reveals why the *femme fatale* remained one of the potent symbols of the period. Mata Hari would pay the penalty for representing the same archetype.

The problem with sadistic killers like Jack the Ripper was that they defied conventional methods of detection, since there was no connection between killer and victim. Fortunately, the age of scientific criminology was about to dawn, with Bertillon's "anthropometry" and Sir Francis Galton's work on fingerprints. Forensic pathologist Bernard Spilsbury, who made his name in the Crippen case, aroused intense admiration because he seemed to be a living version of Sherlock Holmes.

The Crippen case was a landmark for another reason: because he was the first murderer to be caught by means of wireless telegraphy. It must have seemed that, with all these scientific advances, the killer of the future stood little chance of escaping detection. In his utopian fantasies, H.G. Wells looked forward confidently to a crime-free society. But he was reckoning without our incorrigible human tendency to violence. The odd thing about human beings is that even the most unquarrelsome of us is capable of getting irritated beyond measure by some small injustice, and starting a fight. And that is what happened when half a dozen otherwise peaceful nations allowed themselves to be hurled into conflict by two shots fired by a Serbian nationalist. The First World War did for the whole civilized world what the American Civil War had done for the United States: it launched a new era of enterprise and expansion in which crime flourished as never before.

Franz Muller, the Railway Killer, 1864

Muller, the first train murderer, arrived in England from Germany in 1862, and worked as a tailor. Two years later, on 9 July 1864, he entered a railway carriage at Fenchurch Street as the train was leaving for Hackney, and there attacked a prosperous-looking clerk – 70-year-old Thomas Biggs – stole his gold watch and chain, and threw the body out the door onto the line. Biggs died without regaining consciousness. Muller was in such a nervous hurry he left five pounds in Biggs's wallet (then a princely sum) and accidentally took Biggs's hat instead of his own.

A detective patiently checked London jewellers, and eventually located the watch chain in Cheapside. The jeweller, John Death, described his customer as a foreigner, and newspaper publicity about the hat brought information from a man named Matthews, who had bought two identical hats for himself and his friend Franz Muller.

Muller had already fled when the police arrived at his lodgings, but he told another acquaintance that he was leaving for America. Detective Dick Tanner found Muller had embarked on the *SS Victoria* for New York. Travelling by a faster ship, Tanner was waiting for Muller when he arrived; Muller was carrying the missing watch.

Franz Muller was hanged on 14 November 1864, at Newgate Prison.

Franz Muller   27

Lincoln's Assassins are Executed, 1865

previous spread

A crowd witnesses the execution on 7 July 1865 of co-conspirators who aided John Wilkes Booth – assassin of US President Abraham Lincoln. The conspirators were Mary Surratt, Lewis Payne, David Herold and George Atzerodt.

John Wilkes Booth shot President Lincoln in the back of the head during a play at Ford's Theatre, on 14 April 1865. As the fanatical pro-secessionist escaped (by climbing down from the murdered man's box via the stage curtain) he shouted *"Sic semper tyrannis!"* ("Thus always to tyrants").

Initially escaping the authorities, John Wilkes Booth was later discovered hiding out on an isolated Virginia farmstead and was shot dead by Federal troops on 26 April 1865. However, there were rumours at the time that the wrong man had been killed, and the authorities had covered up Booth's successful escape.

Shackled Chinese Prisoners, 1870

The late 19th century was a very turbulent time for the usually conservative and almost changeless China. Between 1850 and 1868, two major rebellions rocked the ancient – and very corrupt – Manchu Dynasty that ruled the Chinese Empire.

In the northern provinces, an army of bandits and army deserters called the Nien set up their own state, while in central China, a fanatical pseudo-Christian army called the Taiping captured the great city of Nanking.

Both rebellions were eventually put down by the Manchu armies, but the estimated loss of life was a staggering 20 million people, most of whom were innocent peasants butchered indiscriminately by all sides.

Following the rebellions, the Manchu rulers attempted to stabilize their weakened position by imposing draconian punishments for the most petty of crimes, but their regime never fully controlled China again.

Janecek the Bandit, 1870

The German mass-murderer Janecek, pictured here shortly before his execution in 1870, led a marauding gang of bandits in Bohemia.

Banditry was becoming increasingly rare in Europe by the late 19th century. While in the Americas and Australia outlaw bandits were enjoying their heyday, European armed robbers found themselves with fewer wilderness areas to hide in and with increasingly sophisticated forces of law and order seeking their capture.

Whereas highwaymen had previously been a threat to travellers on every isolated stretch of road, the advent of the steam train and secure bank safes, not to mention the organization of more effective police forces, made the trade both unprofitable and tantamount to suicide by the time Janecek began his murderous career. The same ineluctable forces also eventually came to bear on American and Australian outlaws, but several decades later than in Europe.

The Tichborne Claimant Scandal, 1873

The shack in Wagga Wagga, Australia, in which butcher Arthur Orton (nick-named "Castro" by the local Wagga Waggans) was said to have dreamed up his fraudulent claim on the multi-million pound Tichborne estate in England.

Orton had heard that Roger, the only son and sole inheritor of the fortune of Lady Félicité Tichborne – an aged widow – had apparently been lost in a shipwreck off Brazil in 1854. Why not go to England, pass himself off as the long lost son and get his hands on the fantastic inheritance?

Orton duly arrived in London and announced his existence to his amazed "mother". Despite being a 26-stone Australian who look nothing like the missing Roger Tichborne, "Castro" managed to convince Lady Félicité Tichborne that he was her long-lost son. On their first meeting, 19 years after Roger's apparent death, Orton lay on a bed in a darkened room and spoke to the wall rather than risk facing Lady Félicité.

The other heirs of the Tichborne estate were less willing to be convinced. On the death of Lady Félicité, they successfully blocked Orton's claim to the multi-million inheritance and a protracted legal battle ensued. After a year-long trial, in which Orton's true identity was revealed, he was convicted of perjury and sentenced to 18 years in jail.

A Brixton Charlie, 1875

London's first policemen were known as the Bow Street Runners because they were founded (in 1749) by the novelist and magistrate Henry Fielding, whose headquarters was in Bow Street. The first Runners were unpaid, relying on rewards for successful arrests. These un-uniformed policemen were supplemented by "Charlies", or night watchmen, like the one pictured in Brixton, London, in 1875.

Founded in 1829 by Prime Minister Robert Peel, the Metropolitan Police (the first uniformed police force in the world – originally nicknamed "Peelers" and "Bobbies") came on the scene so late because public opinion would not tolerate "an internal army". Indeed, for a long time the sight of a policeman being attacked was likely to raise cheers of approval from otherwise respectable passers-by. They eventually became known as "coppers", because they copped (or grabbed hold of) criminals, but it was a long time before the public warmed to the British police enough to treat them as natural allies rather than an arm of a "police state".

Ned Kelly's Suit of Armour, 1880

Ned Kelly was 22 when, in 1877, he took to a life of crime, shooting and wounding a policeman sent to arrest his brother, Dan, for horse-stealing. The Kelly brothers escaped into the New South Wales wilderness and, with two others, set up as bushrangers – the Australian name for outlaw highwaymen and bank robbers. Many poor Australians, suffering under an economic depression and often exploited by powerful landowners, came to see the Kelly gang and other bushrangers as Robin Hood figures.

In reality Kelly was an unlovable thug with a distinctly sadistic turn of mind when it came to lawmen. He seems to have gone out of his way to shoot policemen and, in one case, left one to die of blood-loss after tying him up and cutting off his testicles.

Ned Kelly was finally run to earth in 1880, in the little town of Glenrowan. Kelly, however, was nothing if not resourceful. He emerged from the cabin in which the gang had holed up, firing pistols at the police and wearing a custom-made suit of armour (pictured). Unfortunately for Kelly, he had not bothered to armour himself below the groin, so the police simply shot him in the legs. He was hanged in Melbourne jail on 11 November 1880.

The Clanton Gang, 1881
following spread

Three members of the Clanton cattle rustling gang were killed by the deputized Earp brothers (Wyatt, Virgil and Morgan) and Doc Holliday at the OK Corral shootout in Tombstone, Arizona in 1881. They were, from left to right, Tom McLowry, Frank McLowry and Billy Clanton.

Despite the Hollywood version of the gunfight at the OK Corral, the Clantons were not necessarily the "bad guys". Certainly they were cattle rustlers and bar room hell-raisers, but the Earps were little better. The Earp brothers came to Tombstone with the card-sharping gun-slinger and dentist, Doc Holliday, primarily to make money, not to uphold the law. Some historians now believe that the Earps were simply using their deputized position to gain overall control of Tombstone for their own ends. The gunfight, and the many killings that followed it, may have been more in the nature of a gangster turf-war than a genuine attempt to clean up the town.

ORIGINAL
ARMOUR 14
WORN BY
NED KELLY
The Iron Clad Bushranger

92 lbs
Nº 14

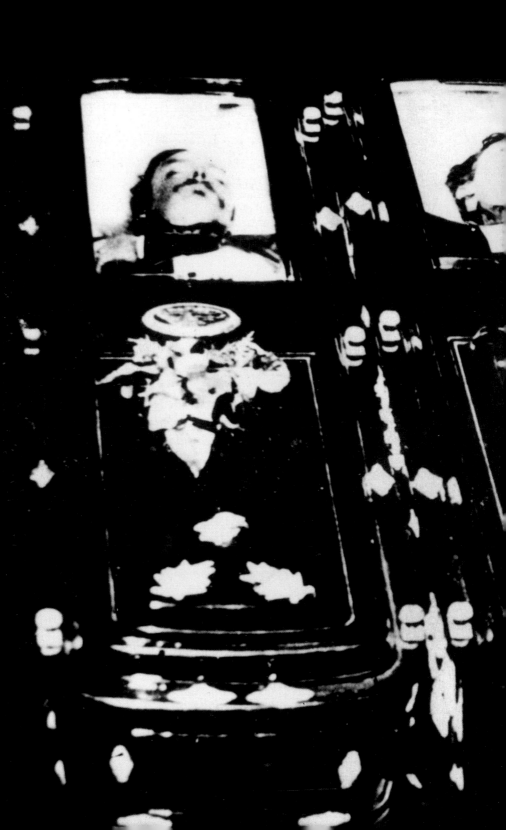

Early Police Investigation Methods, 1884

Police investigation, throughout much of the 19th century, demanded more muscle than brainwork. Here four policemen struggle to restrain a suspect.

Facing a largely uneducated criminal class, a productive inspector usually needed only a network of informants, a good pair of walking boots, a truncheon and a pair of handcuffs.

By the 1880s, however, middle-class, educated crime was on the rise and the need for scientific policing methods came to be felt. The author Arthur Conan Doyle even wrote a number of stories, starting in 1887, seeking to depict the benefits of more intellectual police methods – the hero of these stories was a private criminal investigator called Sherlock Holmes.

Cattle Rustlers, 1885
following spread

Following the chaos of the American Civil War and the rapid expansion of settlers westward, the "Wild West" of the cowboy movies was born.

Originally the name "cowboy" used to have about as much romantic appeal as the term "dairy farmer". Then outlaws realized that a fortune could be made by stealing cows from the cattle barons of the western states. The term "cowboy" first came to mean a bandit, then later took on the gun-toting hard man image (on either side of the law) it has carried to this day.

Irish Poteen Makers, 1885

The Irish have long had a reputation as hard drinkers, but it may have been their habit of drinking poteen (pronounced *po-cheen* – an illegal, roughly distilled potato whiskey) that earned them some of their reputation for being hard fighters.

A County Fermanagh story tells of a local man spotting an English fisherman dipping his bait worms in gin before casting, and catching dozens of trout. The Irishman tells the Englishman he'll try the same trick, but he'll have to use poteen, as he can't afford gin.

The next day the Englishman sees the Irishman carrying home a six-foot salmon.

"By God!" said the Englishman. "I see the poteen worked!"

"Ah, it did indeed," was the reply. "But it took ten minutes to make the worm let go of the fish's throat."

The Pimlico Poisoning, 1886

Thirty-year-old Adelaide Bartlett was accused of murder when her husband was found dead in his bed with an entire bottle of chloroform in his stomach. Police questioning revealed a very odd marital relationship between Adelaide and Edwin, her partner of 11 years.

Edwin, ten years Adelaide's senior, had treated her more as a daughter than a wife, she claimed – refraining from sex and suggesting that, on his death, she should immediately marry his friend, a young Wesleyan minister called Dyson. Adelaide and Dyson freely admitted that they had, on Edwin's instigation, fallen in love. Dyson even admitted that he had bought the chloroform – but both denied hurrying Edwin on his way so that they could carry out his odd request. They said that Edwin had, lately, become lustful of his wife, and had to be coaxed to sleep (unfulfilled) with the anaesthetic. How a whole bottle of the stuff got into his stomach, on the other hand, they claimed not to know.

At the trial, the prosecution could not explain how the searing chemical entered Bartlett's stomach without leaving signs of severe burning in his mouth and oesophagus. Both Adelaide and Dyson were acquitted on the grounds of "a shadow of a doubt".

In fact, a decent medical expert could have told the jury that the lack of burning pointed to murder almost exclusively. The poison could only have been administered via an orogastric tube (down the throat) or direct injection into the stomach – neither of which would have been likely if Edwin Bartlett had either committed suicide or had drunk the chloroform accidentally.

After the trial the surgeon, Sir James Paget, is said to have suggested: "Now that she's acquitted [and could not therefore be re-tried] she should tell us, in the interests of science, how she did it."

Mary Anne Nicholls, 1888

On 31 August 1888 the corpse of prostitute Mary Anne Nicholls was found in Bucks Row. She had had her throat cut and then a long, jagged incision had been made vertically in her abdomen. She is the first known victim of the now infamous serial killer, Jack the Ripper.

Serial murder, as it came to be called in the 20th century, was not unknown to the Victorians, but they viewed it differently before the advent of the Ripper murders. Multiple murderers like Gilles de Rais – the 15th-century, aristocratic child-murderer who became the basis of the Bluebeard fairy story – were well known in 19th-century melodramatic literature. However, the idea that a person could become as addicted to killing people as they could become addicted to alcohol or opium was not then realized. The Ripper murders brought home the fact that a person, apparently sane enough to escape notice in a crowded city, could evidently take pleasure in repeatedly murdering and mutilating total strangers.

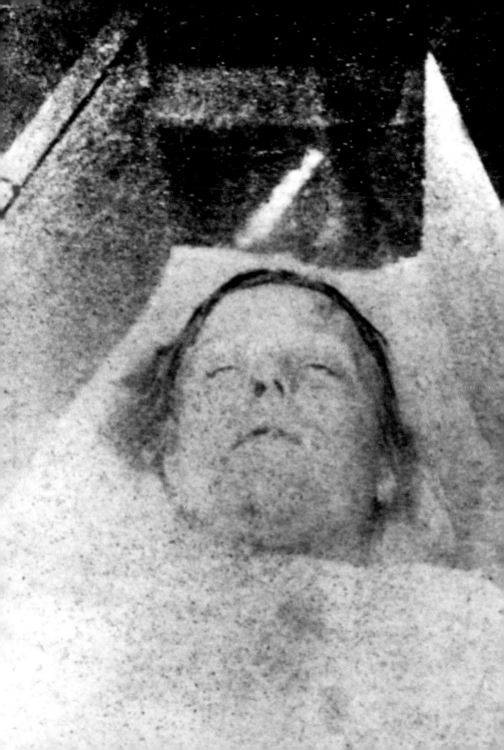

The Jack the Ripper Case, 1888

The streets of Whitechapel formed the backdrop for the series of sex murders carried out by "Bloody-Handed Jack" that horrified Londoners during autumn 1888. In all, five prostitutes were found within a three-month period, all viciously mutilated with a long-bladed knife or scalpel. Someone, claiming to be the murderer, also wrote jeering letters to the press. Although it is by no means certain all (or any) of the letters were from the real Jack the Ripper, one – addressed "From Hell" – contained half a human kidney.

On 7 September 1888, less than one week after the first victim, Mary Anne Nicholls, had been murdered, prostitute Annie Chapman was found dead. She also had died of a cut throat, but as well as slicing open her abdomen, the killer had also carefully removed her intestines and placed them on the ground nearby. She was Jack's second known victim.

Elizabeth Stride, 1888

On 29 September 1888 Jack the Ripper struck twice in the same night. The first victim, prostitute Elizabeth Stride only had her throat cut, so it has been surmised that the Ripper was interrupted before he (or she) could mutilate the body and had to flee. Stride was the Ripper's third victim.

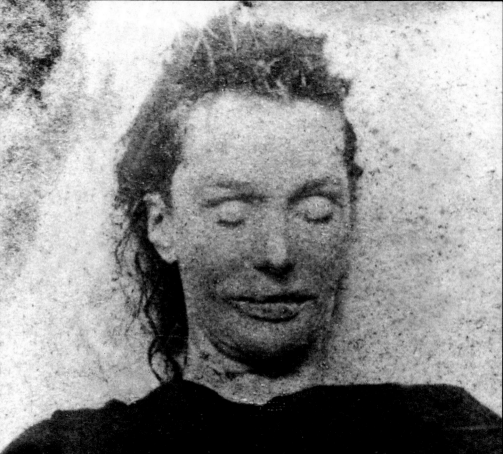

A Mortician's Sketch of the Body of
Catherine Eddowes, 1888

Catherine Eddowes was Jack the Ripper's second victim on the night of 29 September 1888. As well as cutting her throat and disembowelling her, the Ripper also mutilated her face.

The fifth and last murder took place on 9 November. Prostitute Mary Jane Kelly was killed in her own flat (the others were all killed on the streets). Jack cut her throat, hacked her face into a red mess, removed both her breasts, opened her abdomen, filleted all the flesh from her left leg and cut out her heart and burned it in the nearby kettle.

Jack the Ripper was never caught, but recent evidence, found in a diary (apparently dating from the correct period) points to a Liverpool business-man, James Maybrick. Ironically, if this was the case, Jack the Ripper may have ended as a murder victim himself. Maybrick's wife, Florence, was convicted of killing him with arsenic (although as an arsenic addict, Maybrick may have accidentally poisoned himself). Maybrick died in May 1889, just over six months after the last Whitechapel murder.

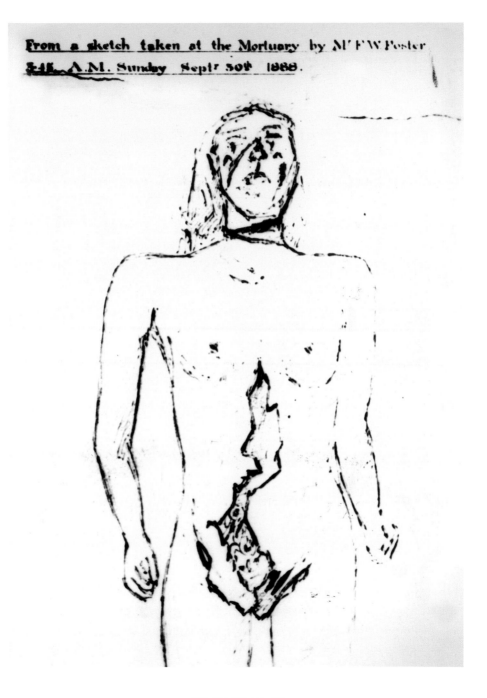

From a sketch taken at the Mortuary by M^r F W Foster
3.45 A.M. Sunday Septr 30th 1888.

The Hampstead Murderer, 1890

Mary Pearcey was a "kept woman" who lived in Kentish Town, north London, supported by a man named Charles Creighton. However, she was in love with a furniture mover named Frank Hogg. Unfortunately, so was Mary's best friend Phoebe Styles. When Phoebe announced that she was three months pregnant by him, Frank Hogg married her but, nevertheless, continued his affair with Mary Pearcey.

On 24 October 1890, Mary Pearcey invited Phoebe Hogg to tea, pressing her to bring "our little darling" – Phoebe's now 18-month-old daughter. During the tea visit, Mary Pearcey struck her rival on the head with a heavy object, then cut her throat. She then wheeled her body in a pram to Hampstead. The baby, who was underneath her dead mother, was suffocated. Mary dumped Phoebe's body and the dead baby in Hampstead on a piece of waste ground.

Frank Hogg seemed largely untroubled by his wife and daughter's disappearance, but his sister Clara went to look at the body in the morgue and recognized Phoebe. Mary Pearcey, who had accompanied Clara, then drew attention to herself by having melodramatic hysterics.

When the police learned that Frank Hogg possessed a key to Mary Pearcey's house they went to search it. They found bloodstains in the kitchen, which Mary – who was nonchalantly playing the piano during the search – explained were due to killing mice. However, she could not explain how the "mouse blood" had got on to her underwear. At her trial the following December, she was found guilty and condemned to death. Her lover, for whom she had committed a double-murder, refused to visit Mary in her condemned cell. She was hanged two days before Christmas, 1890.

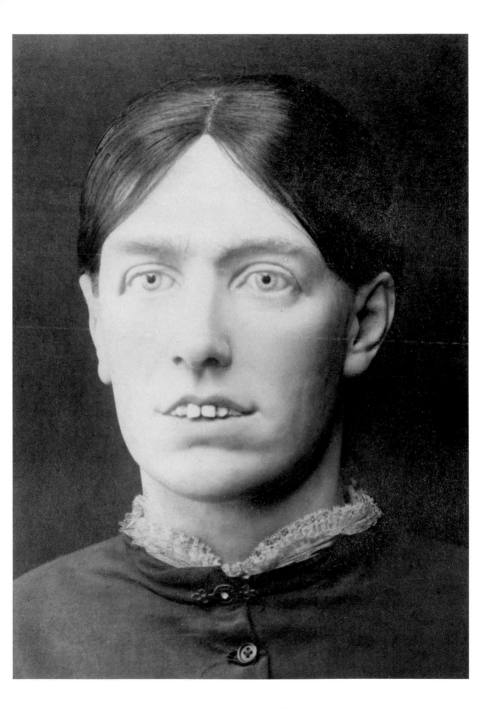

The Dreyfus Affair, 1899

French army officers make their way to testify against Captain Alfred Dreyfus in the infamous spy case of 1899.

Alfred Dreyfus was a French artillery officer accused of selling military secrets to the Germans in the early 1890s. Dreyfus was found guilty and sentenced to life-imprisonment on Devil's Island in 1893.

In fact Dreyfus was completely innocent and had been found guilty largely because he was Jewish. When evidence was unearthed that the spy was actually another French officer, Major Esterhazy, the French military authorities first tried to suppress it, and then arbitrarily acquitted (the non-Jewish) Esterhazy in the hopes that the whole thing might blow over. Dreyfus, needless to say, was left on Devil's Island.

By 1899, however, the Dreyfus Affair had become an internationally reported scandal. The French public were furious when the appeal by Dreyfus failed, despite the overwhelming evidence that he was guiltless.

Faced with the potential fall of his government, the French Prime Minister hurriedly pardoned the Captain Dreyfus, who returned home to his old job in triumph. He was, rather ironically, awarded the Legion of Honour (effectively for surviving the anti-Semitism of his own superior officers) and served with distinction during the First World War.

Execution at Sing Sing, 1900

Execution by electric chair came about because penal reformers were revolted by some rather messy hangings that had taken place in New York State. (If the noose was placed incorrectly or the rope was set too long, the victim was liable either to strangle slowly to death or to die in a shower of gore as their head was ripped clean off.)

Thomas Edison, who invented a direct current (DC) generator, tried to ruin his rival George Westinghouse, who used alternating current (AC), by hiring a showman to electrocute animals with AC to demonstrate how "dangerous" it was. (Of course, AC is actually safer than DC in almost all circumstances.)

Unfortunately the idea caught on, and a murderer named William Kemmler, who had killed his mistress, was the first victim of "the chair" in Auburn, New York, in 1890.

It took so long for the AC current to kill the unfortunate Kemmler that he was virtually cooked, and his hair had caught fire before he finally expired.

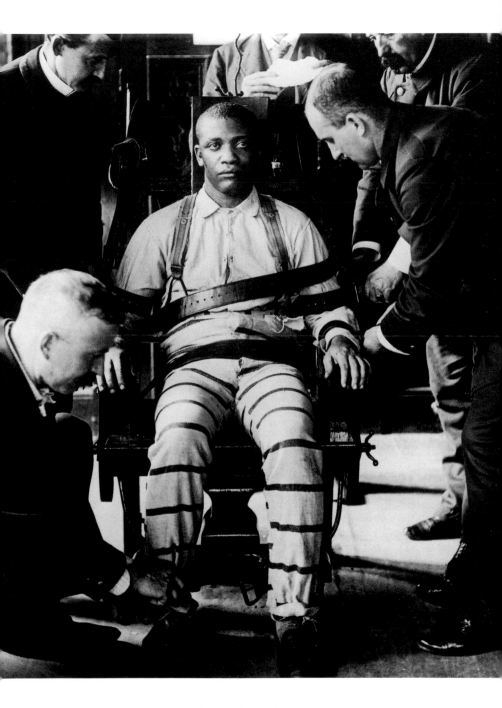

Tenement Complex, 1901

Bottle Alley, a slum district in New York and a breeding ground for crime.

Crime rates increased markedly in the industrial world during the 19th century, especially in rapidly growing cities like London, New York, Berlin and Paris. A prevalent view among middle and upper class Victorians was that this was due to the "moral laxity" of the poor, and many missionary ventures were set up in slum areas.

It would be unfair to say that the Victorians failed to recognize that crushing poverty and non-existent social services might drive otherwise honest people to crime – socialist reformers like Karl Marx, Bernard Shaw and H.G. Wells were vociferous on the subject – but a large section of the better-off in society preferred to ignore the terrible environment that bad pay and foul living conditions created among the urban working class.

An example of Victorian hypocrisy may serve to illustrate the thinking of the time. In 1885, the campaigning British newspaper editor, W.T. Stead, bought ownership of a child prostitute as you might buy a dog. He did this with little difficulty and at pitifully little expense.

Of course, Stead did so to illustrate to his readers the appalling situation for poor children in the London streets, but the reaction of much of the British public was furious and indignant. Stead received death threats for even daring to mention such a distasteful subject in a family newspaper. Parliament was shamed into raising the age of consent, but Stead was also jailed for three months for "abducting an unmarried girl under 16 without the consent of her parents" – a trumped-up charge, as the girl's mother had in fact given her consent.

Casque d'Or, 1902

Two street gangs operated in Paris at the turn of the 19th century. Both referred to themselves as *Apache* – after the warrior people of the American southwest – and sported bell-bottom trousers, caps and polka-dot scarves to indicate their gang membership. The leaders of the two gangs – Leca the Corsican and Manda (known as *"l'Homme!"*) – were rivals in love for a beautiful singer called Amélie Hélie (pictured) – nicknamed *Casque d'or* because of her beautiful red-gold hair.

The rivalry ended in a bloody street fight on the Rue des Haies, with gang members wielding knives and pistols. Fortunately nobody was killed. When arrested and questioned by the public prosecutor, Manda *l'Homme!* shouted, "We fought each other, the Corsican and me, because we love the same girl. We are crazy about her. Don't you know what it is to love a girl?"

They were both sentenced to deportation and hard labour, Manda for life and Leca for eight years. Although both men were incarcerated on the island Saint-Martin-de-Ré they refused to speak to each other, except to reminisce over the their lovely *Casque d'or*. She, on the other hand, was of a more practical nature. Amélie Hélie used the national fame the story generated to further her singing career and to bed a series of rich lovers.

One of Leca the Corsican's Apaches later approached Amélie in the nightclub where she sang and stabbed her in the chest. She survived, but her singing career was over. She died in obscurity in 1933, and achieved posthumous notoriety in the 1950s when the celebrated French director, Jacques Becker, filmed the story under the title *Casque d'or*.

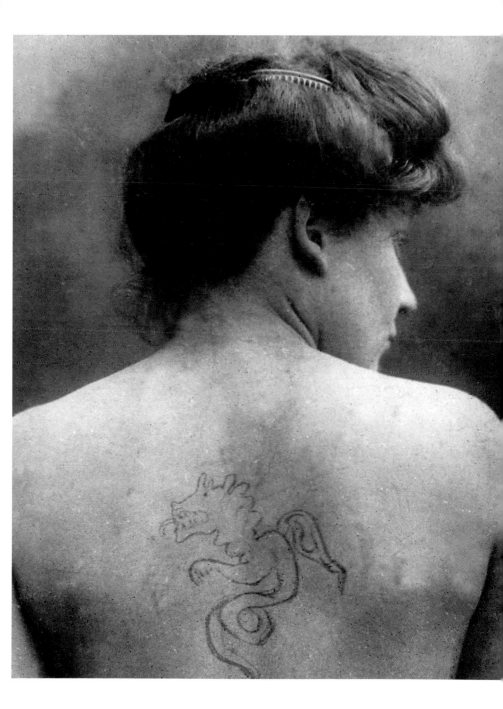

Suffragette Arson Attack, 1903

The modern image of the early 20th-century Suffragette movement tends to be of selfless women protesting for equal rights, even at the risk of imprisonment by the unfair and patriarchal state. Many feel sympathy for Suffragette Emily Davidson, who threw herself under the George V's horse at the 1913 Derby – killing herself and the horse – and thus becoming the first British suffragette martyr (although many feminists, at the time and later, argued her self-sacrifice was an act of supreme idiocy). Unfortunately, like most freedom movements, the Suffragettes also had a violently radical wing, whose actions are harder to sympathize with.

St Catherine's Church in Hatcham was set ablaze (pictured) by Suffragette arsonists in 1903. Ten years later the Surrey home of the leading Liberal politician, David Lloyd George, was bombed – although fortunately there were no resultant fatalities. Political and public condemnation of such terrorist actions did much harm to the movement.

Anarchist Would-be Assassin Mateo Morral, 1906

The dead body of Spanish anarchist Mateo Morral, who threw a bomb at the wedding party of Spain's King Alphonso XIII in 1906. Failing to kill the monarch, Morral promptly killed himself.

Nowadays the term "anarchist" has largely negative connotations – thanks, in part, to hotheads like Mateo Morral. Mainstream party politicians will often describe voluble protestors as "anarchistic" as if the word were a term of abuse but, in fact, anarchism was one of the main voices for social liberalization at the turn of 19th century.

While monarchs and politicians were busily building the socio-military infrastructures that inevitably led to two world wars, men like Francisco Ferrer – an acquaintance of Mateo Morral – were pioneering the Free School movement: schools not only financially free to all pupils, but also free of religious and political control.

Anarchists believed that human beings were fundamentally good and intelligent creatures that did not need to be controlled with excessive numbers of laws and statutes, and certainly didn't need to be "shepherded" by leaders who put the demands of powerful vested interest groups before the interests of their "flock". (An anarchist joke ran: "Shepherds get three things from sheep: wool, meat and, in some cases, sex. What do the sheep get out of the deal? Sheared, butchered and generally screwed.") They were for the most part closer in attitude to the republican libertarians who drafted the US Constitution than they were to Morral.

Evelyn Nesbitt and the Murder of
Stanford White, 1906

The American showgirl, Evelyn Nesbitt, who managed to marry a millionaire – the playboy Harry Thaw. She became the catalyst for murder when her husband discovered that she had committed adultery with the celebrated architect Stanford White. Although never proved in court, it seems likely she egged her husband on to kill White, telling Thaw that White had "violated" her.

Harry Thaw shot Stanford White to death on the open-air roof theatre of New York's Madison Square Garden in 1906. The murder was rather hysterically (and prematurely) labelled the "crime of the century", by the press. Thaw claimed at his trial to have killed White for "violating the innocence" of his ex-showgirl wife. He was eventually found "not guilty" for reasons of insanity and sent to a mental institution.

Stanford White Murder 73

Marie Tarnovska, 1907

Marie Tarnovska, born O'Rourk, was raised in Russia, and eloped with one Count Tarnovsky. He took mistresses and Marie took lovers, two of whom (including her husband's brother) committed suicide for love of her.

Marie, a scheming nymphomaniac, tired of one particular lover, Guards Officer Alexis Bozevsky, and by screaming and pretending she was being raped, induced her husband to shoot and kill him. Her husband learned the truth and abandoned her. But Marie quickly took another lover, Count Paul Karmarovsky.

Soon tiring of Count Karmarovsky as well, she induced Dr Nicholas Naumov, the Count's best friend, to kill him – offering him a passionate night of love as a reward. She persuaded Karmarovsky to insure himself for 20,000 pounds and to make her the beneficiary in his will. Another lover, lawyer Donat Prilukov joined the plot, agreeing to arrive with police and arrest Naumov immediately after the murder.

The Karmarovsky Murder, 1907

On 3 September 1907, Dr Naumov shot Count Karmarovsky in bed in his holiday villa in Venice, after which incompetent doctors completed the job by allowing Karmarovsky to die of his wounds. The maid's description of Naumov led to his arrest as he was fleeing Italy (pictured). He implicated Marie Tarnovska and Donat Prilukov, and they were extradited from Vienna.

Prilukov's legal skills delayed the trial until March 1910. The jury agreed that Marie and Naumov were not entirely sane. Naumov received two years, Marie eight, and Prilukov – who was clearly sane – ten years. In the end, Marie was released for health reasons after two years, became a cocaine addict, and died in Paris in 1923. Naumov and Prilukov died soon after their ruthless lover.

Texas Lynching, 1907

Louis Higgins is hanged by a lynch mob from a bridge in 1907.

The word "lynch" – meaning to torture and execute a suspected felon (usually by hanging) without due process of the law – was coined after Charles Lynch, a Virginia planter, summarily executed a number of loyalists to the British during the American Revolution.

Although mob violence has been common throughout history and in every culture, lynching has been most associated with the US, and most directly connected to the suppression of rights of non-whites. For example, between 1882 and 1951, 4,730 people were reported lynched in the US (although the actual figure is probably much higher). Of these, 1,293 were white and 3,437 were black or Asian.

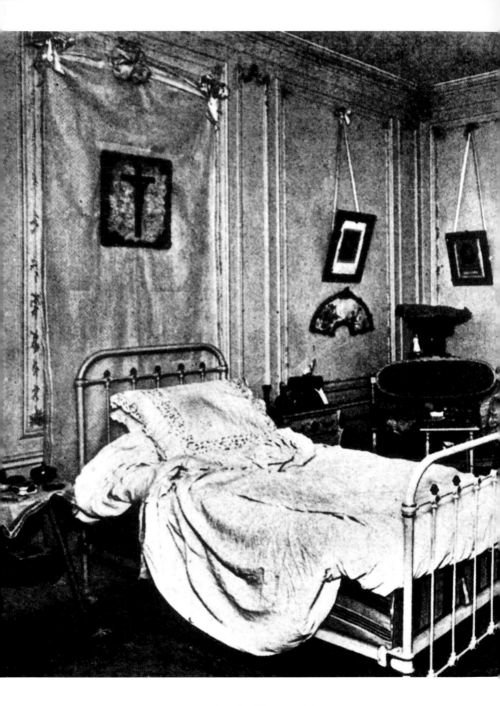

Marguerite Steinheil's Bed, 1908
previous spread

In 1890, a short, cross-eyed French painter named Adolphe Steinheil married an attractive 21-year-old girl named Marguerite (Meg) Japy, and a daughter, Marthe, was born in 1891. Steinheil was not commercially successful, so his wife made ends meet by taking lovers and persuading them to buy her husband's paintings. In 1899, one of these lovers, French President Felix Faure, died of a heart attack while making love to her.

On the morning of 31 May 1908, the manservant Rémy Couillard heard Meg screaming, and found her tied – rather loosely – to her bed. In the next room, Adolphe Steinheil lay dead, strangled with a cord. Meg's mother, Mme Japy, also lay dead nearby, a cotton-wool gag in her mouth. Meg claimed that four burglars, three men and a woman, had attacked them and stolen her jewels. She would later, implausibly, also accuse Rémy Couillard of the crime.

The Steinheil Mystery, 1908

The Steinheil mystery thrilled the Parisian public. For example, who had stopped the grandfather clock in the hall soon after midnight, and why? Was the mother murdered? Is it possible she died of fright while being bound and gagged? It all simply failed to make sense.

The great fingerprint expert Alphonse Bertillon investigated the case, and found that a fingerprint found on the cognac bottle in the bedroom was identical with one found in another part of the house, implying that Meg's faithful maidservant Mariette Wolff may have been involved, and possibly Mariette's son, Alexandre. Both had an alibi – they had been away visiting Bellevue that night – but could easily have travelled to Paris and back that night without being noticed.

The truth was never reached at the time, but the most likely solution to this frustrating mystery is that the servants Mariette and Alexandre Wolff burst into the bedroom in disguise, strangled Steinheil and tied up Meg's mother, then gently tied the compliant and conspiring Meg to the bed.

Steinheil Arrest, 1908

Inconsistencies in her story led to Meg Steinheil's arrest, and it became clear that she was a habitual liar. Her jewels, it turned out, had simply been sent for repair. Meg was charged with lying to the police and obstructing justice. However, the examining magistrate was one of her ex-lovers, so he naturally concluded that she was innocent.

Evidence about the bedroom in which Meg had been tied up figured largely in her trial, which began on 2 November 1908. She tried the court's patience severely with hysterical outbursts, which only served to undermine her credibility still further. It seemed plain that she had somehow been implicated in the murders, but the great problem was that obviously someone else should have been in the dock beside her.

In spite of the suspicions everyone held about her, Meg Steinheil was acquitted on 13 November 1908, largely because the jury could see no possible reason why she would murder her mother.

Meg Steinheil fled to London, and eventually married into the British aristocracy, becoming Lady Abinger. She died in Brighton in 1954.

The Assassination of King Carlo I of Portugal, 1908

On 1 February 1908, both Carlo I and Crown Prince Luis Filipe – the King and the heir to the Portuguese throne – were killed as they drove in an open-topped carriage through Lisbon. The angry crowd immediately caught and lynched the assassins (pictured) so the full reasons for the murders were never discovered, but republican fanaticism seems the most likely reason.

The Portuguese monarchy survived only another two years. In 1910, the country was rocked by a republican revolution and the last king of Portugal, Manuel II, was forced into life-long exile.

Dr Crippen, 1910

Harvey Hawley Crippen, whose name became a byword for horror, was in actual fact a mild-mannered quack doctor. His first wife, a nurse, died of apoplexy in 1892. He then fell in love with a flamboyant actress called Kunigunde Mackamotzki, whose stage name was Cora Turner. Crippen persuaded her to marry him, but soon found that her sexual demands wore him out.

Convinced she would become a great opera singer, Cora took singing lessons that rapidly drained her husband's resources. They moved into 39 Hilldrop Crescent, north London, from where Cora, endlessly and mercilessly critical of her husband, took a series of lovers.

Crippen is Caught, 1910
following spread

Seventeen-year-old Ethel Neave joined the ear specialist's firm Drovet's where Crippen worked, as a receptionist in 1903 when he was 41. A self-pitying girl who was nicknamed "Not very well thank you", she helped Crippen set up a new business when Drovet's went bankrupt through incompetence. They were soon in love, and Crippen was wondering how he could get rid of his wife.

Crippen decided to poison Cora with the vegetable poison, hyoscine. She disappeared on 1 February 1910, and the next day Ethel moved in. Crippen told acquaintances that Cora had run away with a lover, and later announced that she had died in Los Angeles. Cora's friends nevertheless became suspicious and talked to Scotland Yard. However, Inspector Walter Dew was totally convinced by Crippen's admission that his wife was still alive and living with her lover in Chicago. Then Crippen made his fatal mistake: he decided to flee to Canada, with Ethel disguised as his son.

The police soon discovered Cora's dismembered body in the cellar of 39 Hilldrop Crescent, and the manhunt was on. Crippen and Ethel were aboard the SS Montrose, whose captain recognized Ethel as a female and the pair as Britain's most wanted couple. He radioed: "Have strong suspicion that Crippen London cellar murderer and accomplice are among saloon passengers".

Arrested by Dew in Canada (the SS Montrose is pictured arriving), Crippen was tried at the Old Bailey in October 1910, and found guilty; Ethel, tried separately, was found not guilty. Crippen was hanged on 23 November 1910 and a photograph of Ethel placed in his coffin.

Crippen Case   89

Rafael Lopez, 1913

Life in the western United States was becoming more civilized by the end of the first decade of the 20th century, but it was still far from totally safe. Indeed, it is arguable that the outlaw bandits of the late 19th century were the direct forebears of 20th-century mobsters like Babyface Nelson and Al Capone. The early 20th century was merely the transition period from the age of the six-shooter to the age of the tommy gun.

A notable example was outlaw/mobster Rafael Lopez, photographed here in Utah in 1913. The photographer evidently failed to get Lopez' permission before taking the picture, as Lopez shot and severely wounded him moments after the picture was taken.

Police Ambush a Corsican Bandit, 1914

The mountainous terrain of the island of Corsica has always favoured banditry. Indeed, Corsica is one of the few European nations still to suffer the depredations of kidnap gangs in the modern day.

The comic travel writer, Jerome K. Jerome told the story of an English vicar, holidaying in Corsica at the turn of the 19th century, who was kidnapped from his inn during the dead of night.

The vicar was taken to a remote cave in the mountains and there shown a bandit leader, dying of gunshot wounds. The bandit moaned that he had no money, but that he would pay for his final absolution with a piece of advice that would serve the holy man well for the rest of his life. The vicar, both frightened and embarrassed, listened to the bandit's confession and blessed him. Then, with his dying breath, the Corsican whispered his invaluable advice: "Never strike overhand. Always put your thumb along the top of the blade and drive the knife up, under the ribs."

Henriette Caillaux, 1914

On Monday 16 March 1914, Henriette Caillaux, wife of French Finance Minister Joseph Caillaux, walked into the offices of the Paris newspaper *Le Figaro*, and shot journalist Gaston Calmette – whose column had been attacking her husband for weeks – four times (a fifth shot missed). Calmette died that night. The scandal was tremendous, and Caillaux handed in his resignation.

Tried in July 1914, Mme Caillaux pleaded that the gun had gone off accidentally (five times). It's hard to imagine that anyone in France believed her, but no one much liked journalists either, and she was acquitted. Her husband went back into government, only to be imprisoned by Premier Clemenceau for treason two years later. Henriette died in 1943.

The Shot that Rang around the World, 1914

Gavrilo Princip, a young Serbian student, was arrested for the assassination of the heir to the Austro-Hungarian Empire. Princip is shown here with a very bruised face and a broken nose, following several days' police interrogation.

Serbia had been a geo-political football between the Austro-Hungarian and Russian empires for almost half a century. The frustrated Balkan nationalist movement saw the visit of Austrian Archduke Franz Ferdinand on 28 June 1914 – a Serbian national holiday – as a calculated insult.

Earlier that day Nedeljko Cabrinovic, one of the five conspirators who plotted with Princip to kill off Archduke Ferdinand, threw a bomb at the open carriage in which the Archduke and his wife were riding. They both escaped unharmed, although several onlookers were injured in the blast.

Later, the Archduke's open-topped car took a wrong turning in the crowded streets of Sarajevo. As it stopped to turn around at an intersection, Gavrilo Princip stepped out of the crowd and killed Ferdinand and his wife with two shots from a revolver.

Princip was subsequently executed in prison, before the ultimate consequences of his action had taken shape.

Franz Ferdinand's Bloodstained Jacket, 1914

The corpses of Franz Ferdinand, Archduke of the Austro-Hungarian Empire, and his wife Sophie were returned to an outraged Austria for a state funeral, following their assassination by a Serbian nationalist. Ferdinand had predicted his murder shortly before the event, gloomily saying: "The bullet that will kill me is already on its way."

Serbian investigation showed that members of the student political group, Young Bosnia, had conspired to assassinate Archduke Franz Ferdinand. Unfortunately, Austrian investigation also discovered that high officials in the Serbian government had known of the murder plot, but had apparently done nothing to stop it. The Serbian refusal to hand these officials to the Austro-Hungarian Empire for interrogation sparked a declaration of war, which in turn led to the First World War.

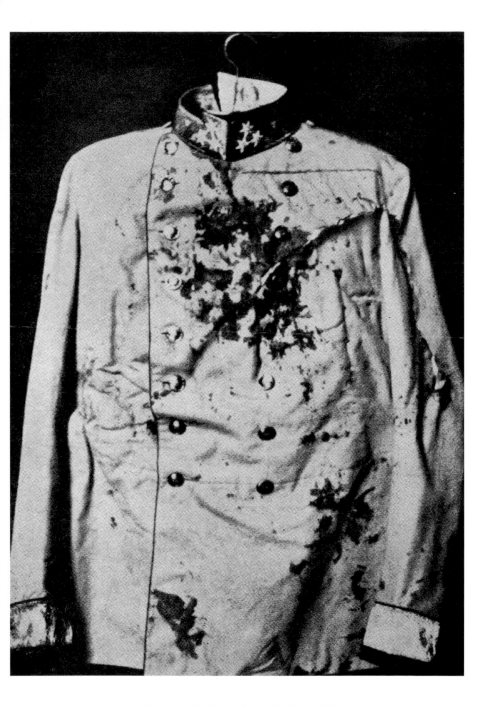

Mata Hari, 1917

Margarete Geertruida Zelle, better known as Mata Hari, is remembered as the archetypal *femme fatale* secret agent. The truth, however, was that she was an adventuress who simply dabbled in espionage. There is little proof that she was ever an accomplished spy.

After the failure of her marriage, in 1905 Margarete Zelle took the name "Mata Hari" and presented herself at aristocratic-but-*risqué* parties as a Hindu princess, trained in exotic – near naked – temple dances. She took France, and later Germany, by storm. If any guessed that she was, in fact, a middle-class Dutch woman, they kept their mouths politely shut.

During the First World War, after more than ten years of celebrity and numerous rich lovers, Mata Hari found herself in financial difficulties and ignored by the paying public (she was now in her forties, although still attractive). In 1916 she seems to have light-heartedly agreed to spy on French military dispositions for the Germans, but if she actually did any spying for the money she received as an advance, there is no surviving evidence. She was detained in Paris on 13 February 1917, and was handed to the military authorities.

Mata Hari was shot by a French military firing squad for espionage on 25 July 1917. Many felt, then and later, that she was unjustly executed. Although it seems certain that she accepted the offer to spy for Germany, her accusers presented no trustworthy evidence that she had done any spying.

The Arrest of a Suspected Spy for the Germans, 1918

The most common sort of spy in the First World War was simply a man or woman who attempted to locate and record enemy troop movements. If they had been issued with a uniform, they were classed as "scouts" and, if caught, were simply sent to a prisoner-of-war camp. If, on the other hand, they were caught in civilian clothes (or the uniform of their enemy) they were classed as a spy by the Geneva Convention. This crime carried the death penalty.

The First World War was the first European war to see mass enforced military conscription utilized by both sides. Desertion and espionage became major problems for the military authorities as a direct result. Enforced soldiers were more likely to run away and infiltration of such large, ungainly armies by enemy agents was all too easy.

Marked as a Spy, 1918

During the First World War, espionage became a key strategic weapon for the first time. Previously frowned upon by military authorities as "dishonourable", spying took on a new importance as thousands died each day, often because generals were simply ill informed of their enemies' strengths and weaknesses. Vigilance against spies became an international obsession (the British MI5, for example, was not formed until the First World War) and suspected spies were treated with contempt and often brutality.

A Frenchman suspected of being a German spy (pictured) has been forcibly tattooed with a Prussian Eagle to mark him for life.

Execution of a Spy at Bois de Vincennes, 1918
following spread

During the First World War, many deserters, enemy agents and traitors to the Allies ended their lives at Bois de Vincennes, on the outskirts of Paris.

Today it is generally recognized that many of the men shot by firing squad during the Great War were unjustly sentenced – sufferers of shell shock and post-traumatic stress syndrome. Their odd behaviour, seen as suspicious by their officers, and their apparent acts of cowardice were often simply stress-induced mental aberrations that were completely beyond their control.

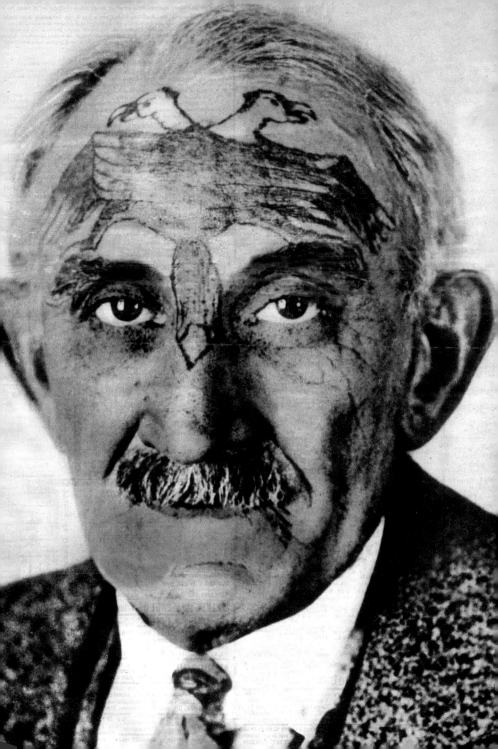

2 THE ROARING TWENTIES AND THE DISMAL THIRTIES

The 1920s were the age of popping champagne corks. Paris and Berlin became cities of sin, with naked dancers and female impersonators. In New York, the writer Scott Fitzgerald rode down Broadway on the roof of a taxi cab and jumped with his wife into the fountain in Times Square. The lovely Starr Faithful carried a flask of cocktails in her handbag, gatecrashed parties, and ended raped and dead on a New York beach wearing only a silk dress. Starr became a symbol of the whole decade – just before the stock market crash brought the party to an end.

In America the party began on 28 October 1919, with the passing of the Volstead Act, one of the most disastrous measures in American history. What Senator Andrew J. Volstead and his "dry" lobby had done was to create in America the same basic attitude that had made Italy one of the most lawless countries in the world: the feeling that Government was the enemy of the people.

By then, the Italian Mafia crime syndicate was spreading all over America. It was known popularly as the Black Hand, and in Chicago, a racketeer named Big Jim Colossimo decided to counter Black Hand threats by sending for his wife's nephew, Johnny Torrio, to protect him – Torrio was a New Yorker. When Colossimo was shot to death in 1920, Torrio became Chicago's crime boss, and sent for a young New York admirer, Alphonse Capone, who lost no time in killing a rival bootlegger, Joe Howard, in a bar in front of witnesses. Oddly enough, the witnesses all developed defective memories, and the police were forced to drop the case for lack of evidence.

And so Chicago, under Al Capone, soon became a symbol of the "roaring twenties" – until Capone made his first great mistake, ordering the killing of six rival bootleggers in the "St Valentine's Day Massacre" in 1929. For Capone, that was the beginning of the end, since President Hoover himself ordered that he be brought to justice.

By comparison with the 1920s, the "thirties" were bleak and threatening. A freezing wind was blowing from Russia, where the first People's Republic had been established in 1917. Karl Marx had foretold the downfall of capitalism through its own inner contradictions, and the Wall Street crash of October 1929 made it look as if his prophecy might be fulfilled. Nine thousand American banks failed, and all over the country, farmers began to go out of business, and many young men, like John Dillinger, Clyde Barrow and "Baby Face" Nelson decided that the banks that were holding farmers to ransom were a legitimate target. In response to this wave of gangsterism, J. Edgar Hoover reinvented the failing Federal Bureau of Investigation, and "G men" (meaning government men) suddenly became the new heroes of the nation.

Since all nations now traded with one another, the American recession soon spread all over the world. And it was German recession, with the unemployed numbering 3 million, that brought Adolf Hitler to power. In Italy, where Mussolini had been dictator since his 1922 "march on Rome", the recession only strengthened his hold on power. In Russia, Stalin would soon confirm his absolute dictatorship with the Moscow show trials, designed to inspire terror in his critics.

The one group in America that appeared to remain unaffected by the bleak scene was America's new crime syndicate, which had now spread all over the country, making its money from gambling, prostitution and drugs. The end of Prohibition in 1933 did nothing to dent their optimism. But, absurdly enough, it was Hitler who finally rescued the world from recession by his invasion of Czechoslovakia, which launched the Second World War.

Landru's Furnace, 1921

Born in Paris in 1869, Henri Desiré Landru was a petty crook and swindler who turned to murder as a way of making a living at the beginning of the First World War. He advertised for brides – targeting widows who had substantial savings – then murdered them and realized their assets. In January 1915, a Mme Cuchet, 39, who worked in a lingerie shop, was living with her 16-year-old son in a villa at Vernouillet together with a man she knew as Diard. Mother and son both vanished. No one is certain how Landru disposed of the bodies, although the likeliest theory is that he burned them in a furnace.

Mme Laborde-Line, the well-off widow of a hotel proprietor, vanished in June 1915, and Landru sold her securities. Next came Mme Marie Guillin, 51, who moved to Vernouillet in August 1915. Landru sold her furniture. In September 1915, Mme Heon, 59, moved into the newly rented Villa Ermitage at Gambais, and vanished. A typist, 45-year-old Mme Collomb, first met Landru in 1915, and went to live with him at Gambais in November 1916; she vanished on Christmas Day. Landru next seduced, then murdered, a poor servant girl called Andrée Babelay, in March 1917, for no clear motive except sex. In August 1917, Landru took Célestine Buisson to Gambais, buying a single and a return ticket; she vanished on 1 September. Later the same month, a Mme Jaume made her first visit to Gambais, and her last in November, Landru again buying a single and return ticket. Victim number ten was a pretty widow of loose morals, 36-year-old Mme Pascal, who vanished in April 1917. The final victim, a lodging housekeeper named Mme Marchadier, went to Gambais on March 13, and vanished.

Landru, the French Bluebeard, 1921

Landru's arrest came about by accident. The families of two victims, Mme Collomb and Mme Buisson, compared notes and led the police to the Villa Ermitage, where they found enough evidence to issue a warrant for Landru's arrest. Soon after, Mme Buisson's sister saw her sister's "fiancé" in the Rue de Rivoli, in Paris, and followed him to his lodging. Landru was arrested on 11 April 1919. His 27-year-old mistress, Fernande Segret, was with him. In the car on the way to the police station, Landru unsuccessfully tried to dispose of a notebook that listed all 11 victims.

Landru's garden and the surrounding countryside were searched without result. Neighbours had noticed an unpleasant black smoke pouring from the chimney of the Villa Ermitage, but only a few inconclusive bone splinters could be found in his cast-iron furnace. Landru was totally uncooperative, declaring that if he were guilty, the police had to prove it. The police found his correspondence with 169 women, but only the 11 victims remained untraceable.

Landru's trial began in Versailles on 7 November 1921 (pictured). Landru's tactic was simply to stonewall, denying everything and insisting that the victims were alive, although he refused to say where. Maître Godefroy led the prosecution while Maître Moro-Giafferi defended. The court was packed, mostly with women, and when one woman was unable to find a seat, Landru stood up and gallantly offered her his own. The stove from Landru's kitchen was shown in court and neighbours of the Villa Ermitage testified to seeing smoke pouring out of the chimney.

Landru, however, remained convinced that he could never be executed unless at least one body was found, and his advocate M. Moro-Giafferi, in a brilliant two-day speech, underlined the lack of proof. Landru was nevertheless found guilty, on the basis of overriding circumstantial evidence, on 30 November 1921. He was guillotined on 23 February 1922. A scrawl, found on the back of a picture in his cell, apparently confessed to the murders.

The Thompson–Bywaters Triangle, 1922

Edith Thompson (centre) and her husband Percy (right) were walking home one evening through Ilford, North London, when a man attacked and stabbed Mr Thompson to death. The assailant proved to be Frederick Bywaters (left) Thompson's close friend and, it was later discovered, Edith's lover.

Fredrick Bywaters insisted he had planned the killing of Percy Thompson without the knowledge of Edith Thompson (indeed, she had screamed for him to stop as he stabbed his old friend). However, love letters to Bywaters from Edith mentioned poisoning her husband. Forensic evidence was produced that showed Percy Thompson had never been poisoned but Edith, nevertheless, went to the gallows with her lover. Popular feeling at the time held that the indignant judge had condemned Edith simply for being unfaithful.

The Teapot Dome Scandal, 1922

In 1921, Republican President Warren Harding transferred supervision of the US naval oil reserve (located at Teapot Dome, Wyoming) from the navy to the Department of the Interior. Harding's Secretary of the Interior, Albert B. Fall, then secretly issued exclusive oil rights to the Teapot Dome reserve to two US oil companies in return for bribes. The scandal was revealed in the Upton Sinclair novel, *Oil!*

The stress of the Teapot Dome scandal did much to cause President Harding's death in office in 1923. However when the case finally got to the courts, only Fall (pictured) was found guilty of wrong-doing. Fall was convicted of bribe-taking, while the oil firms were – oddly enough – not convicted of bribery, despite the evidence that they had paid him the money.

The Crabapple Tree Murders, 1922

following spread

In September 1922, the bodies of Reverend Edward Wheeler Hall (aged 41) and chorister Miss Eleanor Mills (aged 34) were found shot dead beneath an apple tree in New Brunswick, New Jersey. The pair had been lovers, so suspicion fell on Mrs Hall and her relatives.

The only witness who claimed to have seen the murders was pig breeder Jane Gibson. She gave evidence in court, from her sick bed, accusing Mrs Hall as well as Mrs Hall's two brothers and a cousin. The testimony Gibson gave, however, was too inconsistent to hold water.

Fingerprint expert Fred Drewen failed to find incriminating prints on the torn-up love letters found scattered over the murdered bodies of Reverend Hall and Eleanor Mills, so Mrs Hall and the other defendants were acquitted for lack of evidence.

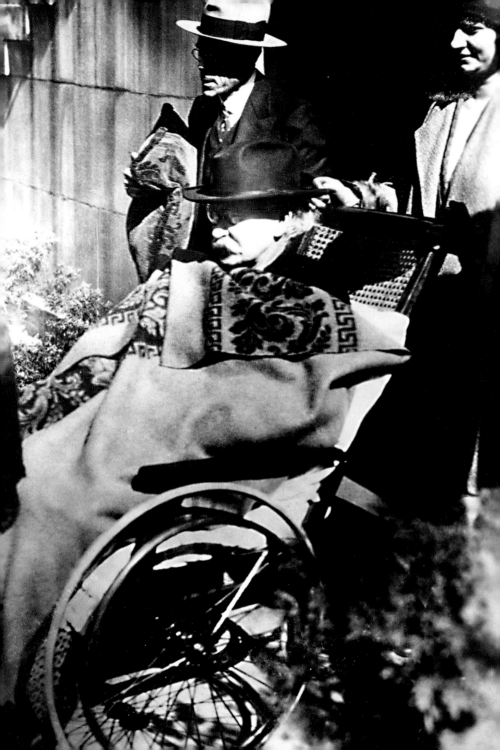

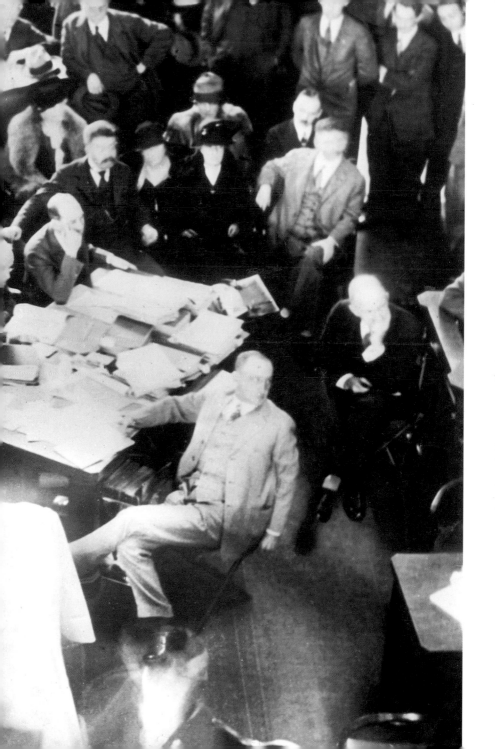

A Cow Shoe, 1922

These two cow hooves were designed to be tied to the sole of a bootlegger's boot. They were to disguise his tracks from investigating customs officials when he was out transporting illegal booze in country areas.

This ingenious ploy was not a 20th-century idea. Cattle-raiders across the Scottish-English border used it for centuries. It is even mentioned in a Sherlock Holmes story, and perhaps this was where the bootlegger got the idea.

Indecency Bust, 1922

previous spread

Chicago women being arrested during July 1922, for wearing one-piece bathing suits. The extra piece of swimwear that the authorities expected them to sport, of course, was a set of leggings or a long skirt to cover their legs.

Decency laws, of course, vary from one generation to another, changing with social attitudes and fashion tastes – but some remain timeless. For example, there is still a North Carolina by-law that prohibits the playing of tennis "while wearing a hat that might startle a timid person".

The Walter Rathenau Assassination, 1922

A poster offered a million-deutschmark reward for information leading to the arrest of the murderer(s) of Walter Rathenau.

Walter Rathenau was a German industrialist, liberal politician and diplomat. A key figure in organizing Germany's economy during the Great War, he was also an important influence on his country's post-war recuperation. In 1922, Rathenau, as foreign minister, signed a mutual recognition pact with Soviet Russia – an act that put Germany back on the stage of international politics.

However, Rathenau was hated by the growing German Fascist movement for his liberalism, his friendly policy towards the Russian communists and, not least, the fact that he was a Jew. He was murdered on his way to his Berlin office on 24 June 1922.

His murderer was never brought to book, but it is strongly suspected that the assassination was carried out by Hermann Fischer – a dedicated fascist. Ten years after the murder, the Nazi government held celebrations to commemorate the killing.

Adolph Hitler and the Beer Hall *Putsch*, 1923

On 9 November 1923, Adolf Hitler led members of the National Socialist Party, later known simply as the Nazi Party, in an attempted overthrow of the liberal Weimar government. The Beer Hall *Putsch* – so-called because it was planned in a Munich beer hall – was an utter failure on most levels. The uniformed fascists broke and ran at the first signs of government resistance, but the subsequent trial of the *putsch* leaders catapulted Hitler to nationwide fame.

Adolph Hitler was not a German, but an Austrian. He had volunteered for the German Army during the First World War and had served with courage but little distinction. Hitler was never promoted past the rank of corporal, because his superiors believed he lacked leadership skills. On the other hand, a senior officer decided to appoint him as an Education Officer – schooling fellow soldiers against the twin threats of pacifism and democracy that the German army felt were undermining the war-effort.

After leaving the defeated army in 1920, Hitler joined the Bavarian National Socialist Party as a full-time activist. Hitler's impassioned speaking style and ruthless force of character led him to the leadership of the party within a year.

The National Socialist Party held populist rallies and terrorized political opponents with threats and beatings, but they soon realized that they could never win power through a mandate of the people. The failed Beer Hall *Putsch* had been a rather desperate attempt to steal power from the reeling Weimar government.

When the coup failed so pathetically, many in German politics thought they had heard the last of the posturing Nazi party.

Adolph Hitler in Prison, 1923

Despite being found guilty of high treason, Hitler served only nine months of his five-year sentence. The democratic authorities did not want to keep Hitler locked up for too long, in case he became a martyr figure to his followers. Perhaps they also hoped that, because the *putsch* had been such a farce, Hitler might be a figure of fun to the German people when he was eventually released. The short sentence suggests that they did not think him too much of a political risk.

During his time in the Landsberg prison, however, Hitler dictated *Mein Kampf* to his secretary, Rudolph Hess. Perhaps the most venomously destructive political document of the 20th century, *Mein Kampf* laid the foundations for future Nazi dominance of Germany and, ultimately, contained the seeds of both the Second World War and the Holocaust.

Murder for Fun, 1924

previous spread

Considered one of the most blood-chilling cases of its day, the Leopold and Loeb case involved two promising and well-off Chicago university students who decided to commit "the perfect murder", for the "intellectual thrill of it".

Nathan Leopold (left) and Richard Loeb (right) kidnapped 14-year-old Bobby Franks near his Chicago home on 21 May 1924, and killed the boy by hitting him over the head with a chisel. They later admitted that they had committed the murder partly to prove themselves "supermen" – after the philosophy of Fredrick Nietzsche, who argued that such supermen were above common human morality.

Following the discovery of the body of Bobby Franks, half buried near some train tracks, Chicago police soon found evidence at the scene that conclusively linked Leopold and Loeb to the killing, including Leopold's spectacles. Police raided Leopold and Loeb's shared flat and found a collection of guns as well as murdered Bobby Frank's shoes and socks – presumably kept as a grisly souvenir. Found guilty of the murder of Bobby Franks, Leopold and Loeb narrowly escaped the death penalty, thanks mainly to the brilliant pleas of their attorney, Clarence Darrow.

Loeb was killed in a prison knife-fight in 1936. Leopold was released in 1958 and spent the rest of his life working as a hospital technician on Puerto Rico. In 1948, Alfred Hitchcock made a film based on the Leopold and Loeb case titled *The Rope*.

Ku Klux Klan Victim, 1924

Nelson Burroughs displays the branded "KKK" on head and chest that Klan members gave him when he refused to recant his Catholicism in June 1924. The Ku Klux Klan was originally a secret movement of vigilantes who, following the American Civil War, handed out rough justice in the Southern United States. The movement disbanded when its leaders saw that it was becoming too violent and corrupt.

The Klan was reborn, decades later, after it was shown in a very heroic light in D.W. Griffiths' 1915 movie, *Birth of a Nation*. The new Ku Klux Klan was savagely racist, sectarian and xenophobic with none of the spirit of upholding justice that founded the original Klan.

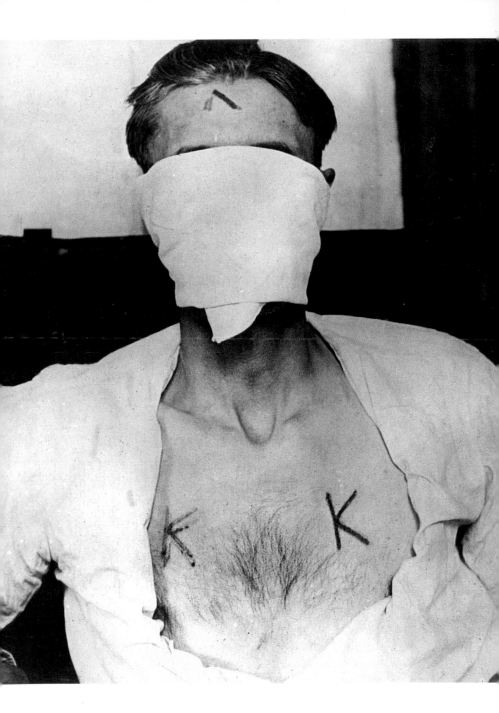

The Cycle Cell, 1925

The road test of the Cycle Cell: an invention designed to allow the Los Angeles Highway Patrol to bring in suspects unaided. It was not a success, partly because the patrolman could not drive around corners at even moderate speed for fear of the whole contraption overbalancing and falling on its side.

Al Capone, 1925

Al "Scarface" Capone was the most infamous American mob boss of the 20th century. Born in 1899, in Brooklyn, New York, of Neapolitan parents, Capone joined a local criminal mob at the age of 11. In 1919, Capone moved to Chicago to act as a strong-arm man in the profitable prostitution trade. It was at this time that he probably contracted the syphilis that would eventually kill him.

By 1925, Al Capone had worked his way up to being the crime boss of Chicago's Southside, running gambling, prostitution, and bootlegging rackets and ruthlessly killing any rivals. His wealth in 1927 was estimated at close to 100 million dollars.

Testing Bullet-proof Armour, 1925

A bullet-proof vest and a bullet-proof face-plate being tested by the German police in the mid-1920s. At the time, new alloys made it possible to stop pistol bullets, even when fired at close range, but reasonably lightweight body armour was not to be invented until the later in the century.

Metal proved to be of limited use in making law-enforcers bullet-proof. Although steel helmets are still used police forces and armies alike, metal body protection has proved too bulky. Also, bullet impacts – although rarely piercing the actual armour – still pass a lot of kinetic force through to the area directly behind a metal plate.

Modern plastic fibre mixes – such as aramid (tradename: Kevlar) – channel some of the kinetic energy away from the immediate impact site, lessening the effect of being shot. They are also, of course, a lot lighter than walking around with a slab of steel attached to your chest.

Opium Smuggling, 1926

A Chinese sailor caught by New York customs officials, trying to smuggle opium into the United States.

Opium smuggling was closely associated with China and Chinese immigrants in the early 20th century, but it should be remembered that opium use was never a part of Chinese culture until the British Empire forced the Chinese to buy vast amounts of the drug in the 19th century. The British even fought two wars (in 1839 and 1856) to break opium embargos set up by the Chinese government.

The Sacco–Vanzetti Case, 1927

following spread

Arguably one of the most shameful injustices in 20th-century American history, the Sacco–Vanzetti case highlighted the problem of racism in US society.

The pair – a fish peddler and a shoemaker respectively – were arrested for committing a payroll heist, during which two guards had been shot dead. Despite very shaky evidence pointing to their involvement, Nicola Sacco and Bartolomeo Vanzetti were found guilty on 14 July 1920, and were sentenced to death. Even at the time, many believed that the pair were found guilty simply because they were both immigrant Italians and card-carrying anarchists.

After four years spent trying to overturn their death sentence, Sacco and Vanzetti had what appeared to be a great stroke of luck. A man called Celestino Madeiros (awaiting the death sentence for another murder) gave a detailed confession to the murders for which Sacco and Vanetti were being held. Despite having this clinching proof that they were innocent, the US Supreme Court refused to overturn the death sentence. The two men were executed on 9 April 1927. Heavily armed policemen stood ready (pictured) during the execution to stop any attempt to rescue the pair.

In 1977, Massachusetts State Governor Micheal Dukakis posthumously exonerated Sacco and Vanzetti.

The St Valentine's Day Massacre, 1929

previous spread

Six members of "Bugs" Malone's North Sider Gang (plus an innocent dentist who just happened to be in the wrong place at the wrong time) were machine-gunned to death on 14 February 1929 in a Chicago garage on Al Capone's orders. A not untypical act of gang warfare in 1920s' Chicago – but the fact that the killing took place on St Valentine's Day won enormous media coverage and made Al Capone a national villain. The police, however, could not link Capone to the massacre.

Ironically Al Capone was arrested only a year later – for income tax evasion. After decades of avoiding arrest on major charges, it had apparently never occurred to Capone to worry about the fact that he was self-evidently making millions, but never paid any taxes.

In 1931 Capone was found guilty of defrauding the federal tax authority, and was given 11 years. He was released on medical grounds in 1939. His mind already rotten with syphilis, he had no chance of rebuilding his crime empire. He died in 1947.

The Düsseldorf Sadist, 1930

Peter Kurten, the "Düsseldorf sadist", born 1883, committed his first murder at the age of nine, pushing a boy off a raft on the river. He spent 27 years of his life in prison, mostly for burglary. Sexually excited by pain and the sight of blood, he began a reign of terror in Düsseldorf in 1929, attacking victims – one man, and several women and children – with a knife, scissors and a hammer. Strangulation also caused him sexual excitement. By the time of his arrest in May 1930, he had committed 11 murders and dozens of sadistic attacks. Beheaded on July 2 1931, he said his dearest wish was to hear his own blood running into the basket

Indiana Lynch Mob, 1930
previous spread

Tom Shipp and Abe Smith are murdered by a white supremacist lynch mob on 7 August 1930. By this stage the Ku Klux Klan had grown, in secret, to monstrous proportions across the US Bible Belt. If the Klan's income had been made public, it would have vied easily with many American major industries. By the mid-1940s, however, the KKK was close to collapse again. The two main reasons for this welcome decline were the public's anger over the Klan's openly pro-Nazi political stance and the fact that the Federal tax authorities had been hounding the movement's leaders for millions in unpaid taxes.

Ma Barker, 1931

Arizona Donnie Barker, known as "Ma", has gone down as one of the more bizarre figures in criminal history. She was a plump, matronly hillbilly woman from the Ozark mountains who, with three of her sons – Herman, Arthur and Fred – travelled around the mid-west between 1931 and 1935, committing bank and train robberies, burglaries, two kidnappings and several murders. (A fourth Barker boy, Lloyd, was also a criminal, but never ran with the Barker Gang.)

Following her death during a shootout with FBI officers Florida in 1935, Ma Barker was built up by the media as the leader of the Barker gang – depicted as planning heists and training her boys in crime – but this was almost certainly pure fiction. There is no proof that she ever even picked up a gun, let alone fired one.

It is true that Ma was deeply dedicated to her sons and certainly did not try to stand in the way of their profitable criminal career, but it is highly unlikely she herself was the gang mastermind. One of the gang members, L.L. Edge, later commented that "the old woman couldn't plan breakfast. When we'd sit down to plan a bank job, she'd go in the other room and listen to Amos and Andy or hillbilly music on the radio."

A more likely reason for Ma Barker's overblown criminal reputation was the then failing reputation of the FBI. During the early 1930s, various failures by the bureau had led to calls for their disbandment. FBI director J. Edgar Hoover seems to have put it about that Ma Barker was a ruthless criminal, mainly to avoid public indignation that his officers had accidentally shot a 63-year-old woman.

The Scottsboro Defendants, 1931

The trial of nine black youths, accused of raping two white "ladies", was one of the major civil rights battles of the 1930s.

On a slow-moving train bound for Memphis on 25 March 1931, nine black youths got into a fight with a group of seven whites who were also "riding the rails", looking for work. The Afro-Americans won, and threw the whites off the train. One of the whites reported the fight, and the order went out to "round up the niggers".

The nine were arrested, as were two white women, Victoria Price, 19, and Ruby Bates, 17, dressed in overalls. Fearing a vagrancy charge, the two women accused the blacks of gang-raping them – although a doctor could find no sign of rape. In Scottsboro, Alabama, they were tried, and eight of the nine were sentenced to death; the ninth, age 13, received life imprisonment.

In the following year the Supreme Court overturned the capital sentences on the grounds that the youths had not been properly represented. Yet even though Ruby Bates had admitted that there had been no rapes, Haywood Patterson, the alleged ringleader, was sentenced to 75 years.

There were loud international protests, including such celebrities as Albert Einstein and author Theodore Dreiser. US consulates were even attacked in Europe.

Finally, charges were dropped against four defendants, and four more were paroled by 1940. Patterson escaped from prison in 1948, but was arrested on a charge of manslaughter two years later, and died in prison.

The Assassination of French President
Paul Doumer, 1932

The dying French President Paul Doumer is loaded into an ambulance on 6 May 1932, having been shot.

Paul Doumer was elected to the French Presidency in May 1931. For the most part a popular politician in his day – set in the grand, 19th-century mould – Doumer had, among other things, served as Governor to French Indochina (an area including, of course, Vietnam).

Considered very successful in this role in his day, it is now generally accepted that the high taxes Doumer levelled on the native population – in the name of making the colony financially self-sufficient, but in reality to pay for the very garrison of soldiers who were enforcing the high taxes – sowed the seeds of deep anti-colonial feeling that eventually led to both the French and American Vietnam wars.

President Doumer's Assassin, 1932

French President Doumer was assassinated by a Russian anarchist, Pavel Gorgulov (pictured). Doumer was 75-years-old and only a week short of his first year in office.

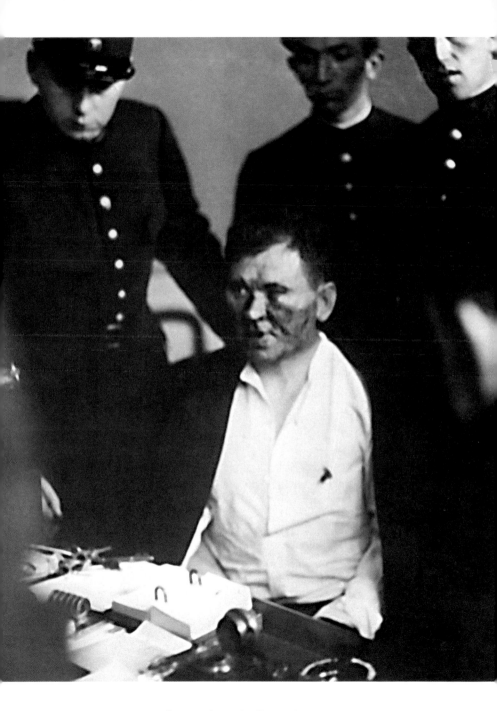

The Lindbergh Kidnapping, 1932

A kidnapping that shocked America took place on 1 March 1932. Toddler Charles A. Lindbergh Jnr was abducted and a staggering 50,000-dollar ransom was demanded for his return. The ransom was paid, but the baby was not returned. The child's corpse was found in woods near the Lindbergh's home eleven days after the kidnapping – he had evidently been deliberately strangled immediately after the abduction.

Charles Augustus Lindbergh, the baby's father, was an all-American hero who made the first solo non-stop flight across the Atlantic in May 1927. Unfortunately, Lindbergh's fame also served to attract a murderous kidnapper to his family.

It was not until September 1934 that police made an arrest in the Lindbergh baby murder case. Bruno Hauptmann, a German immigrant, had tried to pass a note from the Lindbergh ransom money at a Bronx filling station. The serial number was matched with one of those circulated on a list by the police, and the station staff had Hauptmann arrested.

The evidence against Hauptmann was circumstantial, but conclusive. Around 11,000 dollars of the 50,000-dollar ransom was found in Hauptmann's apartment, as was the telephone number of the ransom go-between. A witness claimed to have seen a man, looking like Hauptmann, near the Lindbergh home before the kidnapping took place and, most damning of all, the homemade ladder used to steal the baby (pictured) had been mended with a plank from Hauptmann's attic.

Hauptmann claimed that he was just holding the money for a friend, who had not told him where it had come from. He was found guilty and executed, on 3 April 1936, claiming his innocence to the end.

Clyde Barrow, 1933

Clyde Barrow (pictured) had just finished a 20-month jail sentence for armed robbery when he first met Bonnie Parker (overleaf) who was working as a waitress in a roadside dinner. They became lovers and set up as roaming armed robbers.

Bonnie and Clyde were small-time crooks by the standards of the time, cautiously sticking to robbing gas stations, restaurants and small-town, poorly defended banks. They were certainly not in the league of more daring bank robbers like John Dillinger and Pretty Boy Floyd.

Bonnie Parker, 1933

Despite the distantly small-time robberies that Bonnie and Clyde attempted, the romantic appeal of the pair as gangsters achieved them national fame and an undeserved legendary status. This may have been a key factor in the authorities' ruthless determination to apprehend them, dead or alive.

Bonnie and Clyde were betrayed by a friend and ambushed by police on 23 May 1934. Without even giving warning for the pair to surrender, officers riddled their car with machine-gun bullets, killing both in seconds

Bootlegging Haul, 1933

previous spread

The prohibition of alcohol in the United States began with the Volstead Act in 1919. The act was pushed through congress by a political hegemony of religious fundamentalists, moral crusaders and those people who disliked the increasing urbanization of the USA (cities were generally believed to encourage drinking).

The result was the exact reverse of what the prohibitionists has wanted the ban to achieve. Secret, illegal alcoholism rocketed, criminal mobs of bootleggers virtually ran cities like New York, Cleveland and Chicago and society in general became more, not less libertine. The effect of making a common pastime illegal was to make many feel outside the law, with nothing much else to loose.

Pictured is a warehouse of seized illegal alcohol in New York, in 1933 – awaiting release within the year when President Roosevelt repealed Prohibition

The Stavisky Affair, 1933

In 1933, a Russian-Jewish financier, Alexandre Stavisky operating in France, was revealed as a swindler. Of 640 million francs invested with him, only 14 francs were recovered for the investors. Stavisky's wife, Arlette, was eventually cleared of any criminal involvement, despite having lived a very glamorous life on her husband's embezzled money. Stavisky himself committed suicide (or was possibly murdered to keep him from talking).

The Stavisky scandal shook the French Third Republic. French fascist groups, like the Croix de Feu and Action Française, jumped on evidence that police and civil servants had been bribed to ignore Stavisky's fraud as proof of the overall failure of democracy. Riots broke out in Paris with fascist mob-leaders claiming that Stavisky had been murdered to cover up official corruption. The scandal greatly weakened the already tottering French government, and this could be seen as a factor in their weak reaction to German militarist expansion later in the decade.

John Dillinger as a Boy, 1910

John Dillinger – future "public enemy number one" – aged eight on his father's farm near Indianapolis in 1910.

There is little clue in Dillinger's quiet upbringing to why he later became such a master criminal; from all accounts he was an easy-going, good-natured boy.

At the age of 20, Dillinger joined the US Navy, but found life onboard the *USS Utah* so boring that he deserted after only a few months. Being a deserter in peacetime was not a major crime, but life on the run seems to have set the young Dillinger on the path of petty larceny. He was caught trying to rob a grocery store in 1924 and spent the next three years in prison. It was there that he apparently decided to become a real criminal, and set about learning everything he could about bank robbery from his more experienced fellow inmates.

John Dillinger 171

John Dillinger, 1934

John Dillinger, now officially the FBI's "public enemy number one", aged 31 in 1934.

Dillinger soon became a legendary, even mythical figure in the public's eyes. A brilliant bank robber (who timed heists with military precision) it was also said that no prison could hold him. Indeed, Dillinger once escaped a maximum-security jail wielding a "gun" he had carved out of soap and blackened with boot polish.

Herbert Hoover's newly formed FBI placed its reputation on catching Dillinger (and it is indeed possible that the then unpopular interstate police bureau might have been disbanded if Dillinger had gone uncaught for much longer than he did).

John Dillinger 173

Dillinger Escaped?, 1933

John Dillinger – or a man who looked just like him – was lured into an FBI trap outside the Biograph Theatre in Chicago on 22 July 1934. The authorities said that he was shot dead while resisting arrest, but several witnesses claimed he was shot down without warning. The killing wound, fired at close range into the base of his skull as the man was lying prone on his belly, was what is called an "execution shot" in the military.

However, the fact the man killed outside the Biograph Theatre apparently had different distinguishing marks to John Dillinger (a correct missing tooth, but on the wrong side of his mouth, for example) has led some to believe that the FBI killed a double, and that the real Dillinger used the death to change his face and identity surgically and escape forever.

Whatever the truth to this belief, FBI director J. Edgar Hoover ever afterwards kept a death mask of the man killed outside the Biograph Theatre on his desk as a grisly memento.

John Dillinger 175

Fur Robbery, 1934

A hole bored through a wall into a fur warehouse during a robbery in 1934. A practical necessity in colder climes and a status symbol for the wealthy, furs were decidedly big business for most of the 20th century.

In 1934, the same year as the robbery pictured, The American Fur Company – the foundation of the Astor family's large fortune – was quoted on the stock exchange as the largest commercial organization in the United States.

Little wonder then that criminals targeted luxury fur warehouses for robberies. Unlike gems or banknotes, furs were highly difficult to identify as stolen – especially when they had been incorporated into clothing – so, provided the thieves got away without initially being caught, they ran little risk when "fencing" (illegally selling) their stolen goods.

Improved synthetic and plant fibre clothing, together with the growing animal rights lobby in the industrialized nations, has severely reduced the world market for animal pelts in recent years. When this is linked with the risk of identification of stolen furs through DNA testing, fur robberies must now almost be a thing of the past.

The Brighton Trunk Case, 1934

On 15 July 1934, the rotting body of a woman was found hidden in this trunk in a Brighton lodging house. The victim was identified as 42-year-old Violet Kaye – a vaudeville actress and occasional prostitute. The cause of death seemed to be a violent blow to the head.

Kaye's lover, a small-time crook called Tony Mancini, claimed that he had found Violent already dead at the foot of the stairs to their shared flat on 10 May, and he had hidden her in the trunk because he thought everybody would believe he had murdered her. He had then moved to another lodging house – taking the trunk with him.

The prosecution tried to show that Mancini and Violet had been rowing, and that Mancini had killed Violet with a hammer. However, when the defence showed that Violet had morphine in her body and the stone steps leading down to the shared flat were ill lit, worn and slippery, the jury accepted Mancini's plea of "not guilty".

In 1976, Tony Mancini admitted killing Violet Kaye to the *News of the World* newspaper, safe in the knowledge that he could not be tried twice for the same crime.

Ironically, another Brighton trunk murderer also escaped justice in 1934. On 17 June, a trunk, deposited ten days earlier in Brighton train station, was found to contain the dismembered, headless corpse of a young woman. The victim and her killer were never identified.

Assassination of King Alexander I of Yugoslavia, 1934

King Alexander I of Yugoslavia was a paradoxical political figure. The regal dictator of a police state in his Balkans domain, he was, nevertheless, dedicated to unifying the feuding factions within his country and bettering the lot of the common peasants.

On 9 October 1934, Alexander was on the verge of reintroducing democratic rule in Yugoslavia, and had done much to cement the relations of his new nation with its various neighbours. He was on a diplomatic visit to France – driving through Marseilles with the French Foreign Minister, Louis Barthou – when a lone assassin ran up to the car and shot both men dead.

Alexander I's Assassin, 1934
following spread

The body of Petrus Kaleman, the lone gunman who shot King Alexander I of Yugoslavia dead in a Marseilles street. Although escaping the police and the king's bodyguards, Kaleman was quickly caught and beaten to death by the enraged mob of onlookers. It was later discovered that he had been an agent of the Croatian separatist movement.

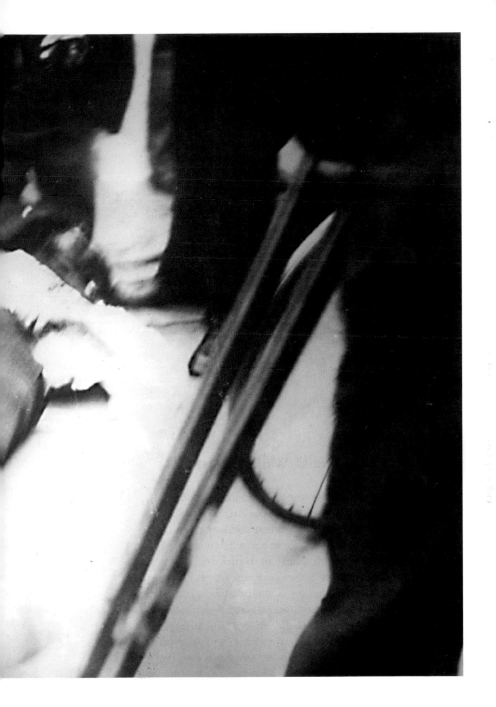

The Walla Walla Prison Break, 1920

Guards in plain clothes tote tommy guns following their successful stalling of an attempted escape from the Washington State Penitentiary, Walla Walla. Thirty convicts captured a human shield of guards during a prison riot, and attempted to march to freedom behind their captives. The group was sprayed with machine-gun fire, killing seven convicts and one guard.

Such brutal use of force to suppress prison riots and foil escape attempts was far from uncommon in 1930s' America. Convict rights were often ignored and guards who killed prisoners were rarely put on trial.

If this sounds inhumane, it should be remembered that 1930s' America was facing a major crime wave, thanks in a large part to the Great Depression, and that US prisons were overfilled with dangerous criminals and ruthless gangsters.

Pretty Boy Floyd and Beulah Ash, 1934

A farmer, driven to bank robbing by the agricultural disaster of the Great Dust Bowl, Charles "Pretty Boy" Floyd won a genuine Robin Hood reputation by also taking and destroying bank debt papers, thus saving many farmers from financial ruin. (Floyd won the newspaper nickname "Pretty Boy" because a farmer, to whom he'd given money, had described him as "kind-faced and kind-hearted".)

Following the death of bank robber John Dillinger on 22 July 1934, Floyd was promoted by the FBI to "public enemy number one". He did not hold the title for long, however. On 22 October 1934, Floyd was gunned down by the FBI while attempting to escape across farmland in Ohio.

Lucky Luciano, 1934

Charles "Lucky" Luciano is now a less easily recognized Mafia figure than Al Capone, but Lucky Luciano was, in fact, a much more powerful boss than Capone ever was.

Starting in petty crime in New York from the age of ten, Luciano soon earned the nickname "Lucky" by escaping arrest and winning crap games. By 1925 he was a second-in-command to a large mob, run by Joe Masseria. In 1929 he survived a mob "hit" when he was repeatedly stabbed with an ice pick and had his throat partially slit open.

Luciano disliked the violence of the ever-present mob wars, largely because it was scaring away business. In 1931, Luciano had Masseria murdered and took over the dead man's gang. By diplomatically cultivating the younger generation of Mafiosi, Luciano became a *capo di tutti capi* ("boss of bosses") and by 1934 had managed to organize a national "crime cartel" – a loose union of Mafia families.

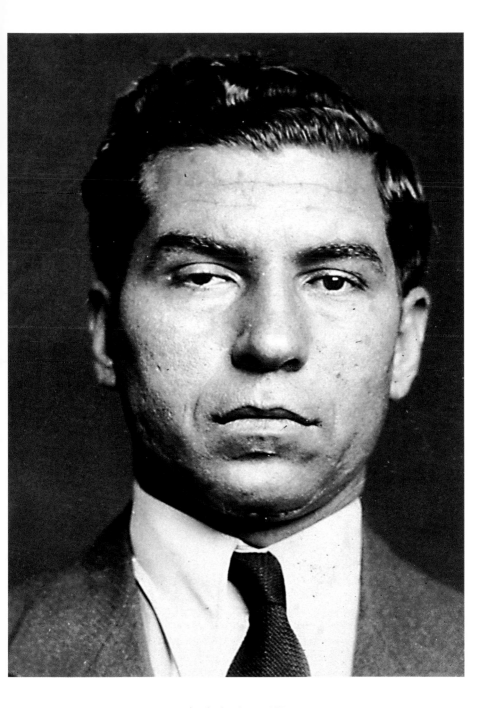

Lucky Luciano 189

Lucky Luciano with His Numerous Lawyers, 1935

In 1935, New York special prosecutor Thomas E. Dewey targeted Lucky Luciano (front, second from left) and gained evidence of his use of forced prostitution: some of the call girls in Luciano's prostitution empire were forced into the life by gangster-pimps. Thomas Dewey found enough of these "sex-slaves" willing to give evidence and the convicted Luciano was sent down for a 30- to 50-year sentence in 1936.

Despite his imprisonment, Lucky Luciano continued to run his crime empire from behind bars. In 1942, he helped the US war-effort by utilizing his mob and union connections to stop sabotage on the New York docks. He was released from jail in 1946 (20-40 years early) partially in thanks for this help. He was, however, immediately deported to his native Italy.

Alma Rattenbury, 1935

In 1935, 38-year-old Mrs Alma Rattenbury and her lover, 19-year-old George Stoner, were tried for the murder of Mrs Rattenbury's husband, 63-year-old Francis Rattenbury. However, the case took an unusual turn.

Francis had been found dying of head wounds at his home in Bournemouth on 25 March 1935. Alma hysterically confessed to the murder, denying anyone else had been involved. Later George Stoner also confessed, insisting that he had acted without Alma's knowledge. Each was evidently trying to take the full blame to save the other from the hangman. During the Rattenbury murder trial, the prosecution sought to prove a case of conspiracy between George Stoner and Mrs Rattenbury. However, George Stoner insisted on taking the entire blame for the murder of Francis Rattenbury and, indeed, the evidence suggested that Alma Rattenbury's confession was untrue. The jury acquitted and released Mrs Rattenbury before, three days later, coming to a verdict of "guilty" on George Stoner.

Convinced that her lover was going to be hanged, Mrs Rattenbury - committed suicide, stabbing herself six times in the chest and heart on the night before his sentencing. She was found where she fell next to the River Stour, near Bournemouth.

Ironically, George Stoner actually escaped the death penalty, having his sentence later commuted to life imprisonment.

A Criminal Impression, 1935

A plaster cast taken from the muddy edge of a French lake. A criminal, escaping from the police, fell and left this impression (note the gun in the left hand). He initially got away, but the police successfully identified him from the imprint and later arrested him.

Police forensics (the scientific study of crime and clues) has made some important discoveries over the last two centuries – although not all techniques have survived the test of time.

In the late 19th century, French police experimented with methods of identification based on the size and shape of a suspect's feet. Identification through anthropometry – the study of the various proportions of different parts of the human body – also showed great promise when it was first introduced. Called *bertillonage*, after its inventor, Alphonse Bertillon, this method soon fell out of use after Sir Francis Galton and Sir Edward Henry found a way to categorize human fingerprints. Although the individuality of fingerprints had long been known, Galton and Henry's method allowed police forces to keep systematically filed records of offenders' prints. This proved to be the single most important development in the science of criminal detection up to the discovery of DNA "fingerprinting" in the mid-1980s.

Sir Bernard Spilsbury, 1935

The most famous pathologist of his time, Bernard Spilsbury was regarded by the British public as the Sherlock Holmes of forensic medicine.

Born in 1877, Spilsbury was a late beginner, qualifying at the age of 28. He became assistant pathologist at St Mary's Hospital, London, but was 34 before the Crippen case made him a household name in 1911.

Crippen, after murdering and dismembering his wife, had fled to Canada with his mistress. The identification of his wife's body – and Crippen's guilt – depended on whether a piece of skin with a white patch was a stomach operation scar, or a piece of skin from the thigh with a fold in it (as Crippen's defence contested). With calm precision, Spilsbury proved that the defence medical expert was talking nonsense.

Other famous cases in which Spilsbury's evidence was crucial included the poisoner, Seddon (1912), the "Brides in the Bath" murderer, Smith (1915), the French butcher, Voisin, who murdered his ex-mistress (1918), the Crumbles murderer, Patrick Mahon, who dismembered his mistress (1924), and the chicken farmer Norman Thorne, who buried an unwanted mistress under the chicken run (1925). But in 1927, it was Spilsbury's evidence on behalf of John Donald Merrett, who killed his mother, that enabled the guilty youth to walk free and to murder his wife and mother-in-law in 1954. Again, in 1943, Spilsbury's evidence on behalf of Harold Loughans, accused of murdering publican Rose Robinson, secured his acquittal; later, Loughans confessed to the murder.

Depressed by the death of two of his sons, Spilsbury committed suicide in December 1947 by gassing himself in his laboratory.

Human Jigsaw Case   198

The Human Jigsaw Case, 1935

previous spread

A crowd outside Strangeways Prison, London awaits the announcement of the execution of Dr Buck Ruxton.

On 19 September 1935, the thoroughly dismembered remains of two women were found in the Gardenholme Linn River in Scotland. Forensics expert Dr John Glaister managed to piece the bodies together and achieved positive identifications. As a result, Dr Buck Ruxton was found guilty of murder of his wife and maidservant. He was executed on 12 May 1936.

A playground song of the time summed up the details of the case (sung to the tune of "Red Sails in the Sunset"):

Red stains on the carpet,
Red stains on the knife,
Oh, Dr Buck Ruxton,
You've cut up your wife.
The nursemaid, she saw you,
And threatened to tell,
So, Dr Buck Ruxton,
You killed her as well.

Dominick Didato's Corpse, 1936

Dominick Didato, also known as Terry Burns, was gunned down in a classic gangland "hit" outside a restaurant on Elizabeth Street, New York in 1936.

Didato had been trying to take over some of Lucky Luciano's rackets while the mob boss was apparently indisposed in prison. The proof that Luciano was still very much in control of his crime empire – even if behind bars – is self-evident.

The picture was taken by the legendary New York news photographer Weegee.

"Machine-gun" Jack McGurn and Wife, 1936

Born in Little Italy, Chicago, James Vincenzo de Mora, the son of an Italian grocer, became a boxer, and changed his name to Jack McGurn. In 1923, his father was murdered by bootleggers. MacGurn gave up the boxing ring and went to work for Al Capone, soon becoming one of his most trusted hench-men. He was one of the killers, disguised as policemen, who took part in the St Valentine's Day Massacre in 1929 when six members of Bugs Moran's rival bootleg gang (and an innocent dentist) were mowed down with machine-gun fire. This brought McGurn's score of murders up to 22. Although he was arrested for his part in the massacre, McGurn escaped conviction.

Machine-gun Jack lay low after this brush with the law. He settled down to running several nightclubs and married the dazzling blonde showgirl, Louise Rolfe, who had provided him with a false alibi for the period he was wielding a machine-gun at the massacre. However, old habits died hard. McGurn later cut the throat of comedian Joe E. Lewis when Lewis refused to work for him; Lewis survived, and his story, *The Joker is Wild*, was subsequently made into a film with Frank Sinatra.

After Capone's imprisonment in October 1931, McGurn's protection and luck ran out. He was soon broke. On 13 February 1936, the eve of the anniversary of the St Valentine's Day Massacre, two gunmen – probably remnants of the now defunct Bugs Moran Gang – caught up with Machine-gun Jack in a Chicago bowling alley and shot him dead with his trademark weapon.

The Lie-Detector Machine, 1937

The polygraph, or lie-detector machine, works by monitoring heart rate, blood pressure and respiration in a subject. A "baseline question" is asked (one that the tester can check is the truth – such as the subject's age or full name) and all subsequent questions are compared to this reading on the graph. Lies usually register a greater reaction than truthful answers.

The polygraph has been used in criminal investigations since 1924, but remains a controversial technique. The physiological reactions measured are supposed to be largely out of human control, but it has been proved that certain individuals can "beat the machine" either through rigorous mental and physical training, or because their natural reactions vary radically from what the polygraph operator is expecting to see.

Most courts, worldwide, refuse to accept polygraph evidence as sole proof of guilt or innocence, and many – for example in Great Britain – flatly refuse to accept lie-detector interrogations as reliable evidence at all.

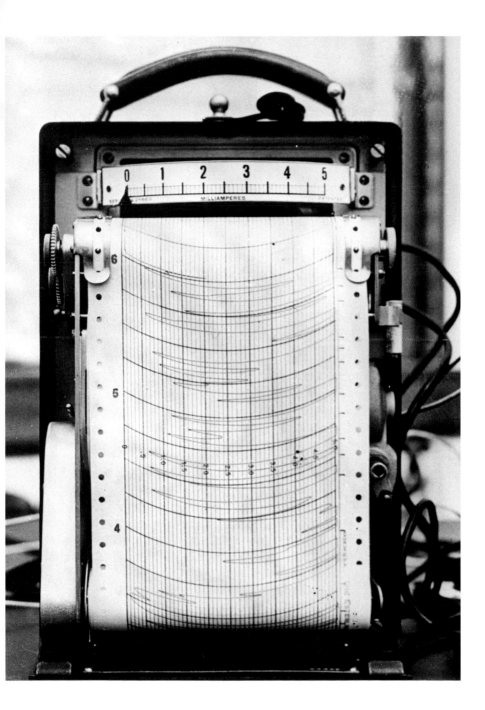

Lieutenant Baillie-Stewart is Released from the Tower of London, 1937

Although not as infamous a Nazi propaganda broadcaster as Lord Haw Haw, or P.G. Wodehouse (who claimed only to have done so under duress), Norman Baillie-Stewart certainly did betray his country in return for Nazi money and German girls.

A Lieutenant in the Seaforth Highlander regiment who graduated from Sandhurst and came from a respected British military family, Baillie-Stewart had a passion for German women and was thereby easily recruited by the Nazi secret service. However, Baillie-Stewart was a terrible spy and soon caught. He spent 1933 to 1937 incarcerated in the Tower of London (the last prisoner ever to be held there).

On his release Baillie-Stewart moved to Germany and eventually won German citizenship. Before and during the war he made a few broadcasts for the Nazis' "Germany Calling" – propaganda broadcast to Britain's radio listeners. He was not as enthusiastic about fascism as he was about German girls, however, and avoided reading the more outrageous scripts provided by Goebbels' Propaganda Ministry.

Baillie-Stewart survived the war and was sent back to Britain. Unlike Lord Haw Haw, the British authorities didn't think they could win a death sentence for Baillie-Stewart, and at one point considered sending him to Russian-controlled East Germany, where there would be no "namby-pamby legal hair-splitting" over shooting him. Eventually, though, he was tried in a British court and sentenced to five years for treason.

Female Burglar under Arrest, 1938

A photograph of an arrested lady burglar in NYPD paddy wagon, taken by New York crime photographer Weegee.

It is a truism, supported by statistics worldwide, that men commit more crime than women – just why this is so, on the other hand, is debatable. Some have argued that men are more "prone" to criminal activity, because they are mentally and physically more attuned to risk-taking than women. Others attack this argument as mechanistic and sexist. It is the social role of women in most societies, they say, that has kept women from competing with men in criminal careers, just as in more laudable activities. Being closeted at home, looking after children, is just as much a hamper to a would-be female cat burglar as it is to a would-be female doctor or lawyer.

Recent statistics and social trends in the developed nations seem to support the latter theory. Female criminality appears to be rising at about the same rate as female involvement in other, traditionally male, careers.

Between 1974 and 1984, for example, the female prison population in Great Britain rose by 75 percent – although, to put this in perspective, in 1984 still only 16 percent of convicted felons in Britain were women. Even though female criminality worldwide is increasing faster than male criminality, it will be a long time before the sexes are on a level of antisocial equality.

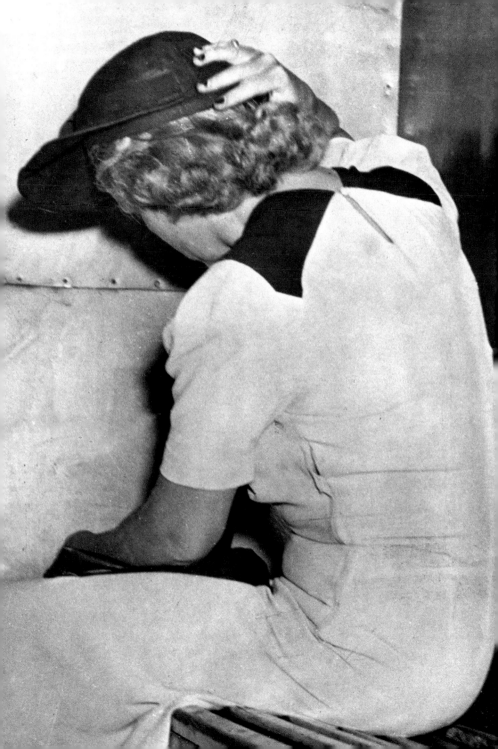

The Von Rath Assassination and the
Kristallnacht, 1938

On 7 November 1938, Herschel Fierel Grynszpan, a 17-year-old Polish-Jewish student, fired two bullets into the belly and neck of Ernst Von Rath, Third Secretary at the German Embassy in Paris. Rath later died in hospital. Grynszpan claimed the murder was an act of political revenge on the anti-Semitic Nazi party.

Ernst Von Rath was given a state funeral by the (secretly delighted) Nazi leadership. The killing of the diplomat was utilized by the Nazi Party's propaganda machine to whip up hate in Germany against Poland (which Hitler was already planning to invade) and Jews everywhere. 9 November 1934 became infamous as *Kristallnacht*, "crystal night", when mobs of Nazi storm troopers smashed the windows and property of German Jews across the nation.

Hundreds of innocent Jews were dragged, without trial, into prison camps on *Kristallnacht*. Many were never seen again. It could be argued that the Holocaust was given its first terrible momentum by Herschel Grynszpan's act of "political revenge".

Eugene Weidmann, 1938

Eugene Weidmann (centre) was a curiously amateurish killer whose crimes seem oddly pointless and motiveless.

The adored only child of a middle-class family in Frankfurt, Germany, Weidmann became a delinquent during the First World War, when he was evacuated to stay with devout grandparents, and began stealing. In his twenties he spent five years in prison for burglary. There he met three future accomplices, named Million, Blanc and Frommer, and they decided to go into criminal partnership in France, renting a villa in St-Cloud, near Paris.

A plan to kidnap a rich American and hold him for ransom went wrong when he fought too hard in the getaway car, and they had to release him. But in July 1937, a second kidnap, that of a pretty New York dancer named Jean de Koven, succeeded. For some reason, Weidmann killed her in the St-Cloud villa, and buried her in the garden. Her traveller's cheques were cashed by Million's mistress, Collette Tricot.

On 1 September, Weidmann hired a chauffeur named Joseph Couffy to drive him to the Riviera; he shot him in the back of the head and stole his car. In mid-October, he and Million arranged to meet a young theatrical producer, Roger Leblond, promising to invest in a show; instead, both shot him in the back of the head and left him in the car, after stealing his wallet.

The fourth victim, an estate agent named Raymond Lesobre, was shot in the head as he was showing Weidmann around a house; Weidmann stole his car and his wallet. The fifth victim, a private nurse named Janine Keller, was offered a job, and driven by Million and Weidmann to Fontainebleau, where she was lured into a cave and killed for her belongings.

Detectives following the clue of a business card left by Weidmann in Lesobre's office found that it led them to the uncle of Fritz Frommer and to the St-Cloud house. Weidmann tried to shoot the detectives, missed five times, and was arrested. He quickly confessed to all the murders, and to that of his accomplice Frommer, whom he accused of being about to betray them to the police.

Weidmann, Million, Blanc and Collette Tricot were tried in March 1939. Weidmann and Million received the death sentence, Blanc 20 months, while Tricot was acquitted. Million's sentence was commuted to life imprisonment and, on June 1939, Weidmann alone went to the guillotine, the last man to be executed publicly in France.

Male Transvestite under Arrest, 1939

A Weegee photograph of a male transvestite arrested by New York police.

The legal position of tranvestitism was a confused issue during the early 20th century in both Europe and America. The act of cross-dressing (wearing the clothes of the opposite sex) was invariably confused with homosexuality, and arrested transvestites were usually convicted under anti-homosexuality laws, regardless of their actual sexual persuasion.

In fact a large proportion of the western transvestite population were and are heterosexual. Most analysts now categorize the urge to wear the clothes of the opposite sex as a form of perfectly healthy fetishism and anti-tranvestitism laws are as derelict as anti-homosexuality legislation in many countries.

Devil's Island Survivor, 1939

Between 1852 and 1939, over 70,000 French criminals were sent to life-long exile on an island off French Guiana, in the Caribbean, nicknamed Devil's Island. Conditions on the penal colony were barbaric and inhuman.

"True", a surviving inmate once admitted, "we [criminals] were devils, but the guards we considered arch-fiends."

The French penal colony was closed down after the Second World War, but for prisoners that survived (pictured) its savage brutality, Devil's Island remained a taint on their lives for ever.

Resisted Arrest, 1939

A Weegee picture of a suspect who resisted arrest. On 18 September 1939, John Pulko was accused of assaulting a woman in Washington Heights, New York. He fled and was eventually captured by two police officers after a wild chase through the streets and a scuffle to get the handcuffs on him.

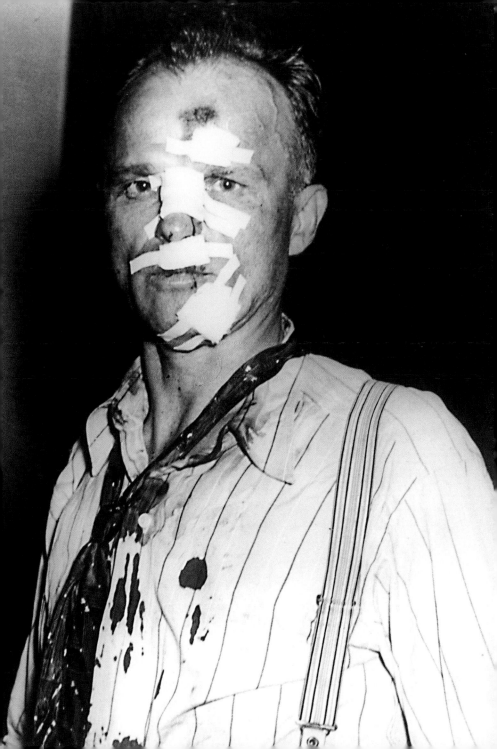

Dead *Boccia* Player, 1939

A Weegee picture of a dead *boccia* (Italian-style bowls) player, shot dead following a heated argument over the game.

After the Execution, 1940

A Weegee photograph of two doctors checking an electrocuted criminal for signs of life.

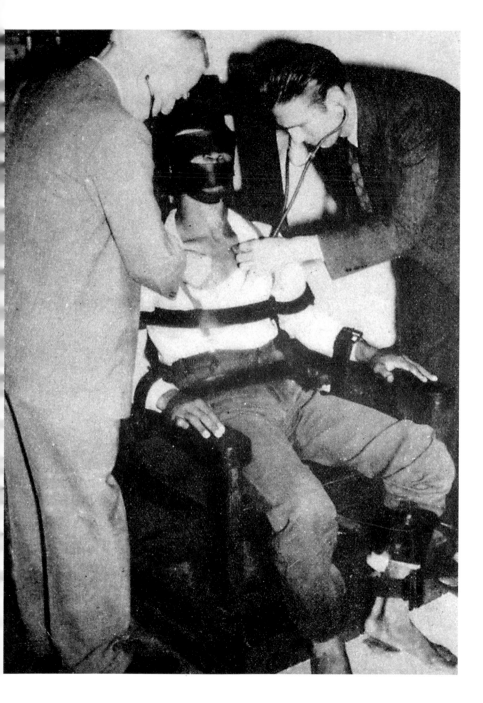

3 WHEN IN WAR-TIME

The murder rate always falls during war-time – partly because so many men are away at the front, partly because when a nation is stimulated by patriotism the criminal urge diminishes.

Although America was not at war with Germany – Hitler declared war on America in December 1941 – spy fever gripped America, since Roosevelt was supplying the British with arms, and German agents did their best to sink the ships while they were still in harbour. The FBI did some of its best work in arresting saboteurs, and the cooperation of Lucky Luciano – who was in prison – ensured that all the waterfront unions joined in the war on the "Fifth Column".

The bombing of Pearl Harbour by the Japanese in December 1941 caused America to declare war on Japan. Four days later, Hitler took the apparently suicidal step of declaring war on the US. This was five days after the Russians had counter-attacked the German army marching on Moscow, which was made possible only because Stalin learned from Richard Sorge – a Soviet, German-born spy living in Tokyo – that Japan had no intention of invading Russia from the east. For the Germans, this counter-attack was the beginning of their defeat.

The Nazis displayed a brutality and ruthlessness that had not been seen since the massacres of Tamurlane in the 14th century. When Heydrich was assassinated by Czech patriots in May 1942, the village of Lidice was chosen at random, and every male in it executed, after which its buildings were destroyed. Thirty thousand French Jews were arrested in Paris, and taken to concentration camps; only a handful survived the war. Millions more Jews died in death camps like Auschwitz and Belsen.

Stalin remained as brutal and paranoid as ever. In August 1941, his agent Ramon Mercader succeeded in gaining the trust of Stalin's former revolutionary comrade Leon Trotsky, who was living in Mexico, and against whom Stalin nursed an old grudge, and stabbed him in the head with an ice pick.

By an incredible piece of luck, Hitler survived a bomb attack in July 1944; many of the conspirators were hanged with piano wire to make their executions slow and agonisingly painful. The Russians, the Nazis and the Japanese broke the Geneva Convention in forcing prisoners of war to work as slave labour. To construct the Burma–Siam railroad, 58,000 lives were sacrificed.

It should also, perhaps, be mentioned that on 13 February 1945, British bombers under the command of Sir Arthur Harris attacked Dresden, a non-military target, in a deliberate attempt to force an end to the war, and 135,000 civilians died in the firestorm. On 9 March US bombers raided Tokyo, and 124,000 civilians died in the firestorm. And on 6 August, an atomic bomb dropped on Hiroshima killed 100,000 civilians. The bomb on Nagasaki three days later was marginally less devastating; it killed 75,000 civilians.

Nuremberg, the city which gave its name to the 1935 Nuremberg Laws, which deprived Jews of civic rights, was chosen as the site of the Nuremberg War Crimes trials (1945-46) in which 22 war criminals were tried. Almost without exception they pleaded that they had simply been acting under orders as soldiers. Göring, Ribbentrop, Keitel, Kaltenbrunner, Rosenberg, Frank, Frick, Streicher, Saukel, Jodl and Seyss-Inquart were sentenced to death. From 1946 to 1948, 28 Japanese war criminals were tried and found guilty; seven were hanged and the rest sentenced to life imprisonment.

But all the while, crime in New York continued to flourish, and was recorded in particular by one remarkable photographer called Arthur Fellig, better known to the city's homicide detectives as Weegee.

Death Camp Experiment, 1940

The crimes of the Nazis were too numerous to be counted, but certainly among the most shocking were the medical experiments carried out in the concentration camps.

Here Nazi doctors have exposed the dead brain of a Jewish prisoner who had first been placed in a low-pressure chamber, then was strangled underwater. The aim of this "research" was to find ways of helping crashed German airmen survive longer in cold sea conditions.

Chief of the death camp doctors was Joseph Mengele – also known as the "Doctor of Auschwitz" and the "Angel of Death". Mengele was especially interested in the genetics of twins, and conducted monstrous experiments on children. Escaping justice, Mengele survived to 1979, when he drowned while swimming near his Brazilian hideout.

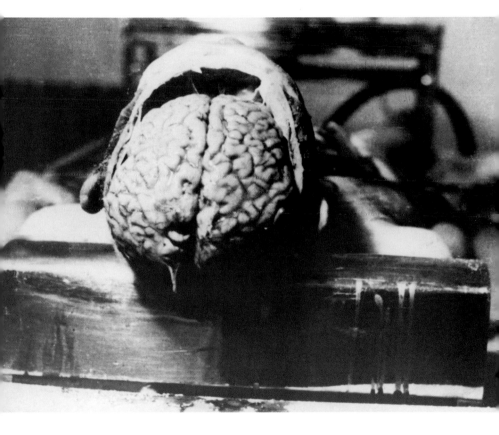

Human Soap, 1940

The astronomical expense of shipping millions of souls across Europe, simply to murder and burn them, annoyed some in the Nazi hierarchy. So efforts were made to make some kind of material profit from the holocaust. Soap was made from the rendered fat of murdered victims (pictured) and the cut hair of death camp internees was woven into a felt-like material to make socks for U-boat crewmen.

The SS also systematically stripped valuables from prisoners before they were gassed (or were worked and starved to death). Although such looting might have gone some little way towards covering the enormous cost of implementing the insane plan of "the Final Solution", the necessity of equipment, guards and rail transport called for by the death camps fatally weakened the German war effort. It is possible that if the Nazis had not implemented the Holocaust, they might have won the war.

A Soviet "Show" Trial, 1940

following spread

As Joseph Stalin, General Secretary of the Soviet Union's Communist Party Central Committee, became ever more paranoid during the 1930s and 1940s, he ordered greater and greater "purges" of political undesirables, counter-revolutionaries and, as often as not, totally innocent men and women.

Most were simply arrested, interrogated, then shot, but high-profile arrestees had to sit through "show trials", where they were forced to give a public confession before being executed.

Stalin "purged" at least 8 million people between 1934 and 1938 alone.

"Fifth Columnist" Arrest, 1941

With the outbreak of the Second World War, the FBI put themselves at the forefront of crushing foreign spy-rings and the saboteurs known as "fifth columnists" (a phrase coined by General Mola to describe saboteurs in the besieged city of Madrid in 1936).

Here an agent is arresting a German spy, Richard Eichenlaub, in New York in July 1941.

One of the most successful Nazi spy busts of the period took place that same year – before America was even at war with Germany. Thirty-three members of a Nazi spy ring were caught and convicted in New York. Typical sentences were 16 to 18 years, but since convicted spies can also be shot under the rules of the Geneva Convention, many Americans believed that the Nazis were getting off lightly.

Allied counter-espionage efforts were so effective during the war that, by the end of the conflict, virtually no Axis spies had escaped detection and/or arrest in either Britain or America.

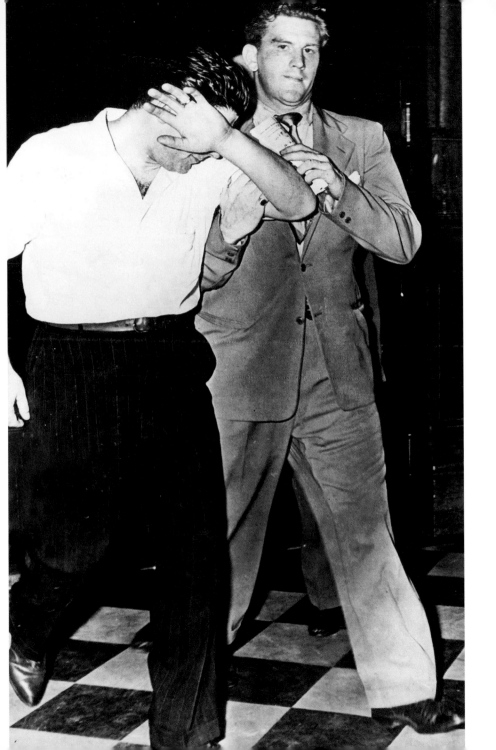

Rooftop Murder, 1941

While the rest of the planet was spiralling into a world war, crime in New York continued as usual. Here detectives inspect the body of Joseph Gallichio, a storeowner shot dead on the roof of his 12 East 106th Street residence, on 14 August 1941. The picture was taken by the famous crime photographer Weegee.

An essential part of Mafia business was the selling of "protection". Legitimate businessmen, like storeowners, paid a regular bribe to the local mob to keep criminals away. This may not sound bad – a sort of private police force – but if the storeowner refused to pay, they definitely would be the victims of crime. The Mafia robbed, committed arson and occasionally murdered those who refused their "protection".

Dumped Body, 1941

A Weegee picture of a young man, murdered and dumped in a New York street. The police tag on his arm reads "D.O.A." – Dead On Arrival.

The American Mafia prided themselves on "only killing their own", meaning that they did not kill innocent bystanders in their turf-wars. In fact, this was far from the truth – spraying machine-gun bullets or tossing hand grenades at enemies tended to injure and kill passers-by – but the US public largely believed the Mafia-propagated myth.

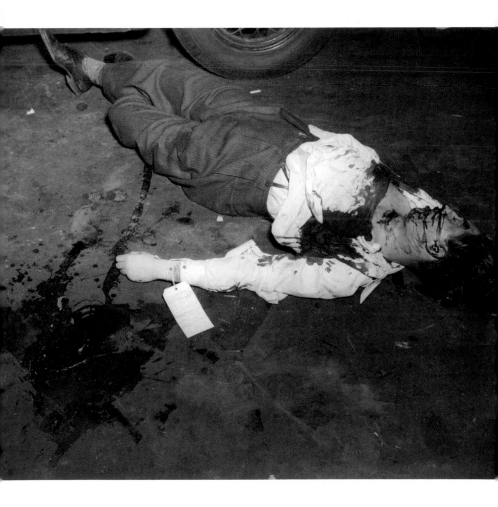

Accused Nanny, 1942

A New York nanny, Irma Twiss Epstein, accused of murdering her newborn charge in 1942.

Killed on the Street, 1942

following spread

A policeman straddles the chalk-outlined corpse of a murder victim outside a New York bar.

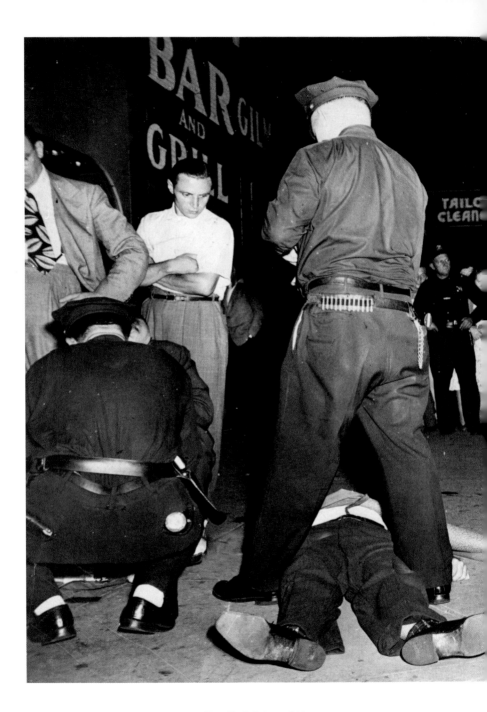

Last Rites for Danny Stanton, 1943

Labour racketeer, and ex-Capone gunman, Danny Stanton is given the last rites following a mob hit on 6 May 1943.

Labour racketeering was an offshoot of the growing power of the labour unions in America. The Mafia simply took over the leadership of a union by election rigging, coercion and bribery. With their own man, like Danny Stanton, holding legitimate power over a union, the Mob could then cream off union dues, launder dirty money through union accounts and blackmail industrialists by threatening strikes.

Of course, despite holding apparently respectable positions, corrupt union bosses were still targets in the occasional mob wars that were a natural part of the Mafia infrastructure in the USA.

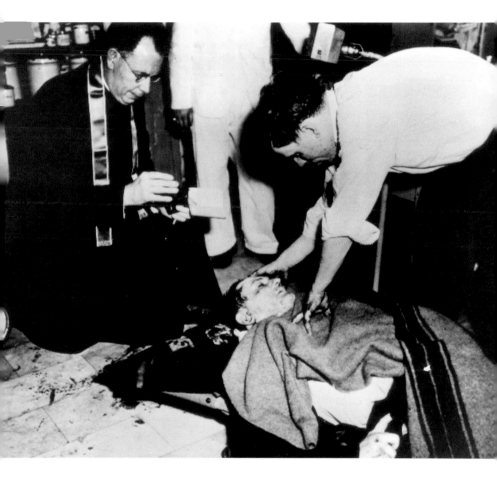

Murder Suspect, 1944

A Weegee picture of a murder suspect. Sixteen-year-old Frank Pape has been accused of abducting four-year-old William Drach, tying him up in a basement and then strangling him.

Nazi War Crimes, 1944

A captured German officer holds up photos of Dutch civilians tortured and murdered by the occupying Nazis.

The Second World War taught the world just how savage war could be. Previous conflicts had been just as inhumane – if not on as wide a scale or with as efficient weapons – but never before had the widespread use of photography and newsreels so thoroughly brought the horror home to the non-combatant public.

Execution by Firing Squad, 1944

A Frenchman, found guilty of betraying his country during the German occupation, is shot after the liberation by the Allies. The picture was taken the moment the firing squad's bullets struck the victim.

Firing Squad   249

Nazi War Loot, 1945

US troops recapture looted art in Germany, for return to the original owners. The Nazis, who banned modern art and jazz music, regarded themselves as highly cultured. So they stole art treasures from nations they conquered and from rich families they sent to concentration camps.

The Allies returned recaptured art treasures, but many irreplaceable master-pieces had simply vanished after the defeat of Germany. Many are believed to have been taken by Nazi war criminals to fund their escapes, and are probably stacked in bank vaults or are hung in private collections to this day.

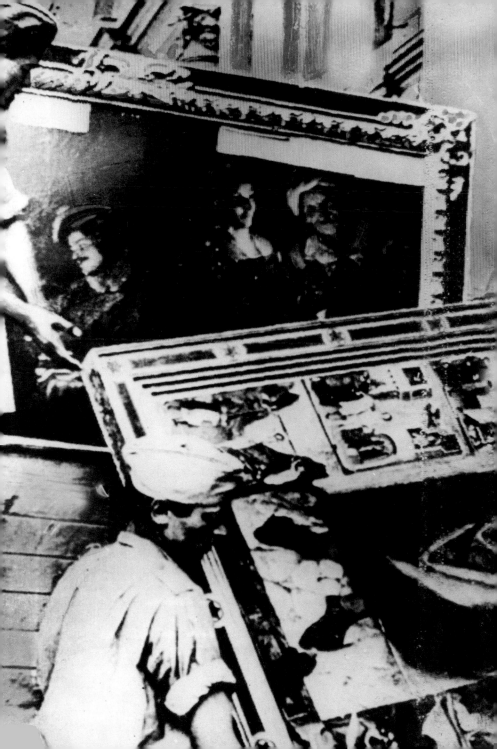

Concentration Camp Guards, 1945

Captured SS camp guards are forced by British soldiers of the 2nd Army to load emaciated corpses for burial at Belsen Concentration Camp.

Jews formed the majority of the victims of the Holocaust, but anti-Nazis, outspoken Catholics, Communists, Gypsies, homosexuals, the congenitally disabled and captured Russian soldiers were also murdered on an industrial scale by the Nazis. Although most were shot or gassed, many were simply allowed to die of sickness and starvation. No final figure can be reached, because the fleeing Nazis deliberately destroyed death camp records, but it is estimated that 6 million people died in the camps, and that a further 2 million died of starvation in Nazi-ruled ghettos, or were shot by roving SS - execution squads. This is a final figure roughly equivalent to the entire population of modern London or New York.

Tokyo Rose, 1945

Iva Ikuko Toguri d'Acquino, also known as "Tokyo Rose".

An American citizen of Japanese parentage, d'Aquino made various English-language propaganda broadcasts for the Japanese under the name Tokyo Rose. After the war she served six years of a ten-year sentence for treason.

Lord Haw Haw, 1945

An American, of Irish parentage, William Joyce made English-language propaganda broadcasts for the Nazis during World War II. He earned his nickname, "Lord Haw Haw", through his sneering tone of voice. Joyce was hanged in 1946 for treason.

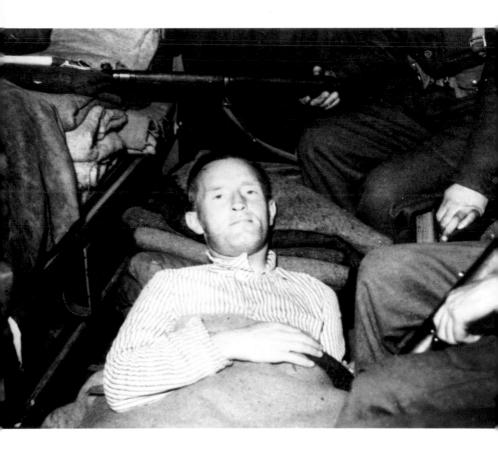

Weegee and a Body in a Trunk, 1945

previous spread

A rare picture of crime photographer Weegee – a.k.a. Arthur Fellig; shown examining a corpse that has been crammed into a trunk and left on a stretch of waste ground.

Fellig won the nickname "Weegee" from New York homicide detectives, because he was always on a crime scene before the other news photographers, and occasionally the police themselves. They joked that he must be using an Ouija board to get scoops from the spirit world. The truth was that Weegee lived and slept in his mobile darkroom in the back of a truck with his radio illegally tuned to the police frequency.

New York Crime Scene, 1945

Residents hang out of windows to watch police investigating a corpse found lying in a shop doorway.

New York's population greatly increased during and after the Second World War. European asylum seekers and Afro-Americans from the Southern States flooded into the city – both groups seeking a life free from the oppression they had suffered at home. New York, always a city made up of national and race ghettos, became even more stratified along racial lines. Resulting tensions often exploded into violence.

Female Drunks, 1945

Inmates wait in the women-only drunk tank in a New Orleans jailhouse.

The new freedoms won by women who left the home to work in essential war industries had the downside that some women used the extra money and free time to become alcoholics. Whereas it was considered normal for men to drink heavily in their time off work, many Americans were shocked that working women might want to do the same.

Although the male sex are still, far and away, the most prone to alcoholic excesses, female alcoholism and drink related crime has been rising steadily since the Second World War.

Bugsy Siegel, 1945

Benjamin "Bugsy" Siegel was a vicious mobster, a thief and professional assassin, but he also had a breadth of vision that surpassed many of his contemporaries.

Siegel looked at the dusty little desert town of Las Vegas, and saw the potential to make millions legitimately, while at the same time secretly laundering large amounts of the US Mafia syndicate's ill-gotten gains. At the cost of 6 million dollars, Siegel built the Flamingo Hotel and Casino in Las Vegas (taking advantage of the State of Nevada's lax gambling laws). This eventually led to Las Vegas becoming "the gambling capital of the world" that it is today.

Unfortunately for Siegel, his criminal habits overcame his long-term vision, and he embezzled too much of the hotel construction money from the Mafia. His partner in business and crime, Meyer Lansky, had Siegel machine-gunned to death through his living room window on 20 June 1947.

At almost the same moment Siegel was dying in a hail of bullets, three of Lansky's henchmen walked into the Flamingo Hotel and announced to the surprised staff that they were now taking over the operation.

Shame-faced Crooks, 1945

A Weegee shot of ashamed arrestees, taken on 25 January 1945. Henry Rosen and Harvey Stemmer cover their faces with handkerchiefs during their arrest for bribing basketball players as part of a betting scam..

War Crime Accusation, 1945

previous spread

A freed Russian slave labourer points out a former Nazi guard – guilty, he claims, of particular brutality.

Apart from the 22 leading Nazis tried at Nuremberg after the war, hundreds of lower-rank war criminals were also jailed or executed on the evidence of their surviving victims.

The Execution of General Anton Dostier, 1945

General Anton Dostier prepares to be shot after being found guilty of war crimes by an American court martial.

Dostier was lucky in one respect: most Nazi war criminals were denied the honour of a military firing squad, and were hanged like common murderers.

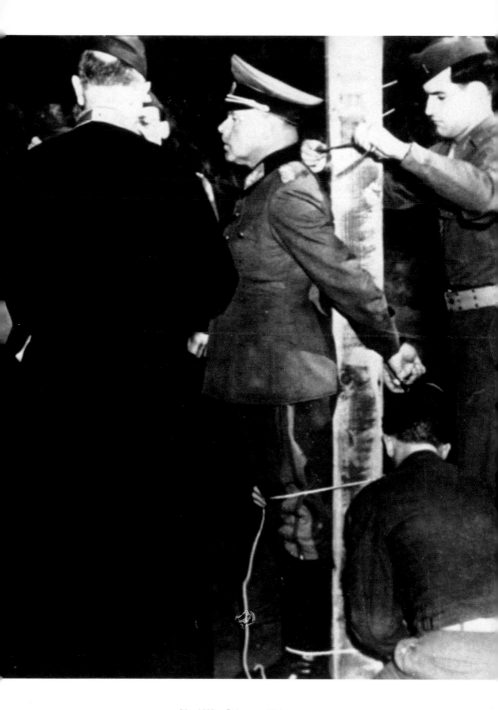

Nazi Holocaust Loot, 1945

Some of the thousands of wedding rings discovered by the US 1st Army in a cave near Buchenwald Concentration Camp, outside Weimar. Each one represents a murdered human being.

SS guards told those being sent to concentration camps to carefully label their confiscated belongings so they could be "sent along later". The idea was to reduce panic as much as possible by creating the illusion that the deportees had a future.

The Nuremberg War CrimeTrials, 1946

Twenty-one of the 22 high-ranking Nazis, tried for war crimes in the autumn of 1946.

Front row, left to right: Hermann Göring (condemned to death, but committed suicide the day before he was due to be hanged), Rudolf Hess (life imprisonment – committed suicide 41 years later), Joachim von Ribbentrop (hanged), Wilhelm Keitel (hanged), Ernst Kaltenbrunner (hanged), Hans Frank (hanged), Julius Streicher (hanged), Walther Funk (life imprisonment – served only ten years) and Hjalmar Schacht (acquitted).

Back Row, left to right: Karl Dönitz (ten years' imprisonment), Erich Raeder (life imprisonment – served only nine years due to ill health), Baldur von Schirach (20 years' imprisonment), Fritz Saukel (hanged), Alfred Jodl (hanged), Franz von Papen (acquitted), Arthur Seyss-Inquart (hanged), Albert Speer (20 years' imprisonment), Konstantin von Neurath (life imprisonment – served only eight years) and Hans Fritzsche (acquitted).

Dead Fascist, 1946

Men cut down the hanged corpse of Fascist leader Nickhazi Janos.

Fascists across Europe had treated their fellow citizens as worthless scum while the Nazis had been pre-eminent. In 1945, with the total defeat of Germany, many paid the price for their arrogance. Some, who escaped trial as war criminals, nevertheless died at the hands of angry mobs.

Hermann Göring in Prison, 1946

Ex-Reichsfuhrer Hermann Göring eats during the Nuremberg Trials in 1946.

Formerly a corpulent opium addict, Göring broke his drug habit, lost weight and put up a spirited defence at his trial. He was, nevertheless, found guilty and sentenced to hang. He forestalled the executioner by taking cyanide (smuggled into his cell in a container of pomade) the night before he was due to be hanged.

Göring had technically been Hitler's second-in-command and designated successor. However, his terrible failures as leader of the German air force (the catastrophes of the Battle of Britain and the Stalingrad airlift were largely due to Göring's braggartry and false promises), his addiction and his dissolute lifestyle meant that he was largely sidelined by more dynamic Nazi leaders like Himmler and Goebbels.

There might be some truth, therefore, to Göring's assertion at his trial that he had not known about war crimes like the Holocaust – that these were entirely the work of the fanatical Himmler. Indeed, some historians have even suggested that Hitler himself, increasingly paranoid and unapproachable even before the war started, had not known of the monstrous excesses of Himmler's SS. Because of the destruction of documentation by the Nazis, the actual truth may never be known.

Hermann Göring   279

The Home-made Gas Chamber Case, 1946

The private gas chamber of French serial killer, Dr Marcel Petiot, was secreted in the floor of his Paris surgery on Rue Lesueur.

Dr Petiot, pretending to be a member of the French Resistance, offered to help Jewish refugees escape from the Nazis. He invited them to his surgery after dark and told them that an escape organization would spirit them to a safe country abroad. Talking them into "hiding" in the secreted cellar, he would seal it up and then gas them, watching their death agonies through a periscope built into the chamber.

Bizarrely enough, the Gestapo arrested Petiot in 1942, on suspicion that he was a member of the French Resistance. He was held until the following year, when he was released without charge. It seems likely that he had confessed his murderous activities under interrogation, but that his equally homicidal captors regarded him as a commendably enthusiastic French supporter of Nazi policies and methods.

The 47 Empty Suitcases, 1946

Forty-seven suitcases were found in Dr Marcel Petiot's Paris surgery. The owners, Jewish refugees from the Nazis, had been secretly gassed, dismembered and burnt by Petiot. The doctor then sold his victims' belongings on the black market. It is estimated that by targeting families trying to escape Europe – who were thus taking all their valuables with them – Petiot's ill-gotten gains ran into six figures.

However, it seems likely that Dr Petiot's main purpose in killing was, like all serial killers, sado-sexual. A colleague later noted that Petiot had quietly sadistic tendencies, and the fact that he liked to watch his victims' death agonies tends to suggest that he was gaining sexual gratification from the murders.

Dr Petiot's Defence, 1946

Dr Marcel Petiot stands in the dock during his trial for the murder of 27 people. Despite the fact that police, alerted in 1944 by the foul black smoke coming from his furnace chimney, had found the dismembered corpses of 27 people in his surgery cellar, Dr Petiot managed initially to brazen the situation out.

He quietly told the French investigating officer that the corpses were traitors executed by the Resistance. Since the Germans were still occupying Paris at that time, the story rang true, and Petiot was released until his claim could be secretly confirmed or denied by Resistance leaders. Of course Petiot promptly vanished with his wife and son.

Later, after the Germans had been driven out of Paris, Petiot made the mistake of writing to a newspaper, claiming that he had been killing Germans not, as was actually the case, families of French Jews. The letter was traced and Dr Petiot was arrested.

Despite putting up a spirited defence – still claiming the murderers had been committed on Resistance orders – Petiot was found guilty and guillotined on 26 May 1946. Although he was only convicted for the 27 corpses actually found in his cellar, Dr Petiot admitted to having killed 63 people before he was executed.

Marcel Petiot 285

4 SPIES, LIES AND MAFIA TIES

With the war over, crime in America went back to business as usual – except that the mob now felt that it had some backing from the US government "for services rendered" in tackling waterfront sabotage; as part of that deal, Luciano was released from prison (albeit to be deported to Italy). Crime boss Frank Costello took the place of Lucky Luciano, and the Mafia expanded further. In Italy, the Mafia felt that its help in the overthrow of Mussolini was virtually a carte blanche to do what they liked.

At the end of the war, Eisenhower had politely permitted the Russians to enter Berlin first, although the Germans had been only too anxious to let the Americans and British take over, if nothing else, to avoid the mass rape of their women. As it was, the western Allies were given West Berlin. In July 1948, Stalin tried to drive them out by blockading road access to Berlin; the Americans responded with an airlift, which lasted ten months before the Russians backed down. But when Mao Tse Tung's communists took over China in 1949, and the North Korean communists invaded the South in June 1950, the west woke up to the fact that Communism was still aiming at world domination. Winston Churchill created the phrase "Iron Curtain" to describe the division that was being created by Stalin.

Innumerable cases of espionage characterized the Cold War period, and led to the immense popularity of the spy novel. Alger Hiss, the Rosenbergs, Klaus Fuchs, were all idealistic "atom spies"; so, in the 1950s and 60s were Guy Burgess, Donald Maclean and Kim Philby. The art historian Sir Athony Blunt was unmasked a decade later.

As always after a war, crime rocketed. By 1946, Britain's crime statistics had doubled, while in America they rose by two thirds. And although the crime figures dropped in the early 1950s, this was only because robberies and burglaries had fallen due to rising prosperity; rape and crimes of violence continued to rise.

England continued to have its celebrated murder trials: Neville Heath (1946), a sadistic killer of women, John George Haigh, the "Vampire Killer" (1949) who dissolved his victims in sulphuric acid, and Reginald Christie (1955), the sex killer who filled a cupboard of his house in Notting Hill Gate with dead naked women.

But the Moors Murderers case and several American cases already suggested a new direction homicide was taking. In 1962, Albert DeSalvo began strangling and raping women in Boston, and was not caught until he had killed 13; in 1966, Richard Speck killed eight nurses in a Chicago hostel. And the murders committed by the Manson "family" brought the 1960s to a violent conclusion.

These were the predecessors of the "serial killers" of subsequent decades – a term coined by FBI agent Robert Ressler, who heard someone speak of a "serial burglar" at a British seminar on crime. They were an ominous herald, in that most of the widely publicized murder cases since then have involved more serial killers.

In addition, the kind of "social protest" indulged in by Manson at his trial provided the prelude to a later growth of terrorism. The "Red Brigades" – German, Italian and Japanese – started from the assumption that capitalist society needed to be overthrown by violence, and that all bankers, bureaucrats and politicians were equally guilty, and deserved to be kidnapped and executed.

Boss of Bosses, 1946

Frank Costello – real name: Francesco Castigli – was the mob leader who took over as the US Mafia's "boss of bosses" when Lucky Luciano was deported in 1946.

In 1951, Costello was indicted to give evidence to the Senate subcommittee investigating organized crime in America. Incredible as it may seem, many government officials at the time (including FBI boss, J. Edgar Hoover) flatly denied the existence of crime organizations in the US, despite the copious evidence to the contrary.

Perhaps over-confident due to this ignorance (or corruption) in high places, Frank Costello refused to co-operate with Senator Estes Kefauver's investigation into organized crime. Costello was found guilty of showing contempt of the US Senate and sentenced to 18 months in jail. While serving, he was also found guilty of income tax evasion and given a further five years. Released in 1956, Costello found his hold on nationwide Mafia power had been usurped by his old enemy, Vito Genovese. Costello later had his US citizenship revoked and was deported to Italy.

Vito Genovese, otherwise known as Don Vitone, also had a hard time as the "boss of bosses". Convicted for drug smuggling in 1959, Don Vitone managed to run his criminal empire from prison for ten years. He died in jail of a heart attack in 1969.

Mob Hit, 1946

Small-time gangster Turi Montalbano lies slumped in his car outside his apartment on 45th Street, Brooklyn, on 20 August 1946, shot dead. The assassin hid in the back of the car and shot Montalbano three times in the head and neck as he climbed into the driver's seat.

Art Forger, 1947

Han van Meegeren, a Dutch art forger, fooled many experts with his brilliant faking of paintings by the 17th-century Dutch masters, Pieter de Hooch and Jan Vermeer.

Van Meegeren was a rich eccentric whose own paintings were well respected. When one of his forgeries was found among the loot amassed by Nazi leader Hermann Göring, it was traced back to van Meegeren, who confessed to painting 13 other forgeries. Nine of these had been sold at enormous profit before the war to legitimate buyers.

Van Meegeren was sentenced to one year in prison, but died of a heart attack before he could start his sentence.

The Black Dahlia, 1947

During January 1947, the corpse of 22-year-old would-be actress and part-time prostitute Elizabeth Short (pictured) was found on a stretch of waste ground in Los Angeles. The naked body of the Black Dahlia – so-nicknamed because she always wore black clothes and underwear – had been cut in half at the waist. Forensic examination showed that she had been hung upside down and tortured before she died.

Although there were 27 fake confessions to the crime, the actual murderer was never caught.

Murder Gang, 1947

previous spread

London crime journalists, nicknamed the "murder gang" by the police, are briefed by Scotland Yard's Chief Information Officer.

The police have sought to use the power of the press to aid investigations since before the days of Jack the Ripper. In many ways, the news media are a police force's main conduit of communication to the general public.

The Acid Bath Murders, 1948

Evidence arrives for the trial of John "Acid Bath Murderer" Haigh.

On 1 April 1948, John Haigh, a petty conman, was arrested and admitted to killing eight people (including an entire family of three). He had disposed of the corpses in a bath of sulphuric acid. Despite his confession, Haigh thought he would eventually go free because, as he told police: "You can't prove murder without a body."

Haigh's method was to shoot his victim then dissolve the body in the acid. He thought this method constituted a "perfect crime" but, in fact, more than enough evidence was left (teeth, for example) to send him to the gallows.

Strangeways Cell Search, 1948

Strangeways Prison warders search a prisoner and his cell for contraband.

The concept of "prisoner rights" is fairly new to human civilization. For most of history, prisoners were considered lucky if they were allowed to live – whatever the conditions.

Initial movements towards prison reform started in Britain in the 19th century, and generally made things worse for prisoners. Eighteenth-century prisons had been squalid and corrupt, but were relatively low on discipline. Victorian prisons were clean and efficiently run, but their aim to reform prisoner's morals made them Hell-on-Earth.

Inmates were kept in solitary cells and were not allowed to speak for the duration of their sentences. They were also made to "work", turning heavily weighted handles all day long, which achieved nothing other than to exhaust the prisoners. This is why prison officers are still derisively called "screws" in Britain.

Prisoner rights are now recognized, to varying degrees, in most countries, but over-crowding and poor management still often makes prisons Hell-on-Earth. The Russian novelist, Fyodor Dostoyevsky, once said that "the degree of civilization in a society can be judged by entering its prisons". By that standard, few modern nations have much to be proud of.

Lucky Luciano in Exile, 1949

Exiled, Lucky Luciano (fourth from the left) maintained his criminal career from Italy, smuggling drugs and illegal immigrants into the USA. He died of a heart attack in 1962, aged 66.

True to his name, Lucky Luciano outlived the majority of his Mafia boss contemporaries.

Arsenic Murderer?, 1949

Frenchwoman Marie Besnard was accused of killing 12 people with arsenic (then available from shops for household purposes). The corpses were disinterred and found to be full of arsenic. However, Besnard's defence council argued that the local soil had infected the buried bodies with arsenic through the action of rare anaerobic microbes found in that region.

After 14 years' scientific testing, in which Besnard was free on "provisional liberty", the theory was declared unprovable either way and the charges were dropped.

Bomb Book, 1950

This time bomb was discovered by New York Police in 1950. The two sticks of gelignite are enough to level a medium-sized building.

Although unconnected with the above discovery, New York was to suffer further, apparently random bombings in the early 1950s. The "Mad Bomber", as the newspapers called him, left home-made bombs in Grand Central Station, Radio City Music Hall, Macy's department store and several other public places. Fortunately nobody was killed in the resulting explosions, but this was down to pure luck rather than to the bomber avoiding casualties.

A letter, claiming to be from the bomber, denounced the Edison Electric Company for causing his tuberculosis. It was then a simple matter to check company records for ex-employees who had made such a claim.

The trail led to George Metesky: a respectable 54-year-old bachelor ... with a bomb factory in his cellar. Metesky was found to be clinically paranoid and spent the rest of his life in a mental hospital.

Giuliano the Bandit, 1950
following spread

Salvatore Giuliano, the renowned Sicilian bandit and kidnapper, lies dead outside his hideout in the village of Castelvetrano.

After a seven-year manhunt the police finally cornered Giuliano on 7 July 1950. He preferred to try to shoot his way out of the trap, rather than surrender – a decision that cost him his life.

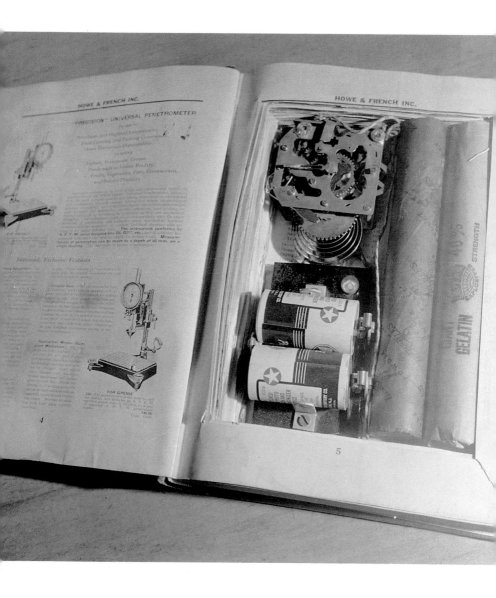

The Kray Twins, 1950

Ronnie and Reggie Kray, twin brothers born in 1934 to Violet Kray (centre) in the East End of London. The Kray brothers were to become two of the most feared gangsters in the city by the mid-1960s.

Initially starting out as professional boxers, the Krays soon moved into the mob "protection" rackets. Their success was mostly due to their willingness to indulge in the most extreme violence but was also coupled with a sly sort of cleverness.

For example, when Ronnie was incarcerated in a mental institution in 1956, Reggie went to visit him. When visiting time was over it was Ronnie who walked out. Reggie waited until his brother was well away and then revealed who he really was. The institution authorities had no choice but to let Reggie go.

Despite being disarmingly charming when in the public eye, the Krays – especially Ronnie – could explode into violence on any pretext. Ronnie once gave a friend a slash to the face that needed 70 stitches, simply for making a playful remark about Ronnie putting on too much weight.

Alger Hiss, 1950

In 1950, high-ranking US State Department official Alger Hiss was accused of handing documents to confessed Soviet spy, Whittaker Chambers. Hiss (pictured) denied the charge and was tried for perjury. Future US President Richard Nixon was one of the most vociferous accusers of Hiss. On evidence that Hiss had indeed met Chambers after the date he had sworn to have last seen him, Hiss was convicted and served three years of a five-year sentence.

Hiss' conviction gave great momentum to Senator McCarthy's rabid anti-communist campaign while, on the other hand, Hiss was defended as innocent by the American political left up to 1996. In that year, released Soviet intelligence documents all but conclusively proved Hiss had been a spy for the Soviets. Hiss died in 1996, at the age of 94.

Gaston Dominici Case, 1952

Early on 5 August 1952, a motorcyclist was flagged down by a French farmer, Gaston Dominici, and asked to fetch the police. Dominici said he had heard shots and found a body lying by a Hillman station-wagon. Dominici's farm, Grand' Terre, was nearby (some 30 miles from the town of Digne in the south of France).

The corpse of Sir Jack Drummond, 61, was found shot in the chest. The same fate had been meted out to his wife, Lady Ann Drummond, aged 46. Their ten-year-old daughter, Elizabeth, lay on the other side of a nearby railway track, her skull crushed by two blows with a blunt instrument.

Eventually, after more than a year, 75-year-old Gaston Dominici (pictured re-visiting the murder scene, front right) confessed to the murders. He had seen Lady Drummond undressing and made an advance. Sir Jack defended his wife and Dominici had shot both of them, then clubbed their daughter to death with the rifle butt – the rifle was later found in the river.

The trial, in November 1954, ended with Gaston Dominici being sentenced to death. This was later commuted to life imprisonment, and he was pardoned in 1960, aged 83. He died five years later.

Slick Willie Sutton, 1952

Willie Sutton – also known as "Slick Willie" and "The Actor" – was a master of disguise as well as a highly resourceful bank robber. During his criminal career he twice escaped from maximum-security jails and robbed over 2 million dollars from banks across the US.

Sutton was arrested for the last time in 1952, after a five-year manhunt. He was released from jail in 1969.

Famously, when asked why he robbed banks, he replied: "Because that's where the money is."

Slick Willie   317

Loving Traitors, 1953

On 17 July 1950, US citizens Julius and Ethel Rosenberg were arrested as part of a Soviet spy-ring which had handed western atomic research material to the Russians. The prosecution pressed for execution for Julius, but asked that Ethel – who seemed less involved in the spy-ring – only be given 30 years' imprisonment.

Judge Irving Kaufman, sentencing *both* to die, stated that he believed the Rosenbergs guilty of swinging the course of history to America's disadvantage. He even claimed that their espionage had indirectly been the cause of the recently started Korean War.

Following their treason arraignment, the Rosenbergs kissed in handcuffs. After 20 failed appeal attempts over two years, the Rosenbergs were both electrocuted on 19 July 1953.

John Christie, 1953

On 24 March 1953, a newly arrived Jamaican tenant of the ground floor flat of 10 Rillington Place, west London, removed an area of wallpaper in the kitchen and found a concealed cupboard. On opening it, he was horrified to find the bodies of three dead women. There had been no warning smell of decomposition, because the atmosphere of the sealed cupboard had perfectly dehydrated the bodies.

Suspicion fell on a previous tenant, John Reginald Christie (pictured), as the bodies had evidently been placed there during his stay in the property.

The Rillington Place Murders, 1953
following spread

The interior of 10 Rillington Place revealed not only three dead women in the sealed-off cupboard, but a further dead woman under the floorboards in the front room. The garden also gave up a number of human bones from two more bodies (including a femur that had been used to prop up the fence).

Police searched Christie's flat with a dreadful suspicion in their minds. Four years earlier, in 1949, the bodies of the wife and baby daughter of upstairs tenant, Timothy Evens, had been found in the washhouse of the ground floor flat. Evens – who had the IQ of a ten-year-old child – had been hanged for the murders. But was Christie the actual killer?

The bodies in the garden were the first to have been killed. The three in the concealed cupboard in the kitchen showed signs of carbon monoxide poisoning as well as strangulation. Mrs Christie, like Mrs Evens, had simply been strangled.

A necrophiliac, John Reginald Christie brought women back to his flat, knocked them unconscious with coal gas, strangled them, then had sex with their corpses. Mrs Christie was apparently unaware of her husband's activities – that is, until he killed her too (possibly because she had discovered his secret).

Christie confessed to killing seven women – including Mrs Evens, a crime for which her husband, Timothy Evens, had been hanged (it seems likely that Evens killed his baby, but that Christie was responsible for the death of Mrs Evens). Christie himself was hanged on 15th July 1953.

The Richmond Towpath Murders, 1953

Police search the neighbouring undergrowth and river for clues left by the murderer of two teenage girls.

Sixteen-year-old Barbara Songhurst and her 18-year-old friend, Christine Reed, went missing while bicycling along the River Thames towpath, near Richmond, west London on the night of 31 May 1953.

Alfred Whiteway, a 22-year-old labourer, initially being held by police for attacking and raping a 14-year-old girl, became a murder suspect after Barbara and Christine were found in the river. They had been raped, then stabbed and hacked to death.

Whiteway first confessed to raping and killing the girls, then retracted his statement and pleaded "not guilty" at the subsequent trial.

When it was revealed that Barbara Songhurst had known Whiteway – thus giving him a motive to kill them both after raping them, to stop them from accusing him – the jury convicted him and he was hanged three days before Christmas, 1953.

Ruth Ellis, 1955

On 10 April 1955, a night-club hostess, Ruth Ellis, fired all six shots from a revolver at her lover, racing-car driver David Blakely, outside the Magdala pub in Hampstead, north London.

Many believed that Ruth Ellis had been mentally unbalanced at the time she killed Blakely, and her defence council tried to persuade her to press for a conviction of manslaughter rather than murder. Ruth, however, seemed determined to die: at the trial, when asked what she had intended to do when she pulled the trigger, she replied: "It's obvious that when I shot him, I intended to kill him."

Ellis was found guilty of murder and murmured "Thanks" as the death sentence was past.

She was the last woman to be hanged in Britain, prior to the abolition of the death penalty.

The Cambridge Spy-Ring, 1955

"The Cambridge Spy-Ring" was a loose term coined by the press to describe the British spies for the Soviets who were unmasked in the 1950s and 60s. Most were recruited while they were undergraduates at Cambridge University.

Kim Philby – photographed (centre) while celebrating his clearance on charges of being a Soviet spy in 1955 – was, in fact, an extraordinarily successful spy for the Soviets. He betrayed British and American secrets from within the British secret service, where he was a high-ranking officer, up to his unmasking and escape to Russia in 1962.

Another member of the Cambridge spy-ring was Donald Maclean. As First Secretary in the British embassy in Washington DC, Maclean was in a position to hand immensely damaging secrets to his Russian controllers. He was eventually unmasked and fled to the USSR with fellow Cambridge Ring member, Guy Burgess, in May 1951.

Anthony Blunt, the last of the Cambridge spy-ring to be caught, worked in MI5 during the Second World War and compromised many of Britain's anti-Soviet counter-espionage operations. After the war he ceased to be a spy and was eventually knighted as the Queen's favourite art expert. Caught in 1964, Blunt was given immunity from both prosecution and public disgrace, in return for a full confession. He was publicly unmasked in 1979 by Prime Minister Margaret Thatcher, and lived in ignominy until his death in 1983.

Tattooed Japanese Gangster, 1955

American administration of defeated Japan imported many western ideas and institutions, both deliberately and accidentally, following the end of the Second World War. They did not, however, import organized crime to Japan: it was there already, and had been for centuries.

The *boryokudan*, meaning "tough gangs", have existed in Japan since the Shogan wars of the 16th century. *Ronin* (masterless samurai) joined together into bandit gangs and extorted food, money and women from the frightened peasantry. Almost 500 years later the modern *boryokudan* are doing much the same, although through extortion, political corruption and prostitution.

Boryokudan members are called *yakuza* – literally meaning "eight-nine-three:" a bad hand in the Japanese version of blackjack, where the aim is not to go over 19. The implication is that gang members are good-for-nothings. Nevertheless, *yakuza* proudly announce their gang affiliation with elaborate tattoos.

Jack "Spot" Comer, 1956

Jack Comer was a London East End mobster and leader of a horse-race betting gang which specialized in absconding with the winnings before they could be claimed by punters. His name became familiar to the British public in 1955, after a quarrel in Soho between Comer and a bookmaker named Albert Dimes. Comer had been trying to slash Dimes with a knife when he dropped it. Dimes picked it up and slashed Comer's face instead.

At the resulting trial, an 88-year-old retired clergyman named Basil Andrews insisted that he had seen Dimes draw the knife on Comer. The jury acquitted Comer, but revealed their doubts about the evidence by acquitting Dimes as well. The Rev. Andrews eventually admitted that he was a racing enthusiast, and had been bribed to testify in Comer's favour. The three men who had bribed him went to prison for perverting the course of justice.

Six months later, Comer was attacked and knocked to the ground with a crowbar. Comer insisted that he had not recognized his attackers, but his wife, who had been present, named a gangster friend of Dimes, Billy Hill. Eventually two of Comer's attackers were caught and sentenced to seven years each.

By that time, however, Comer was already losing his position as one of London's leading gangsters to younger rivals like the Krays.

Jack Comer 333

The Death Switch, 1956

The so-called "death switch", in Sing Sing Prison, New York; placed so that the executioner could see that nobody – such as the priest or administering doctor – was in contact with the condemned prisoner at the moment of electrocution.

Although now abolished in many countries like Portugal, Brazil and Great Britain, the death penalty remains on the statute books in many other nations and a number of states in the USA.

The arguments for capital punishment, leaving aside the vengeance aspect, centre on the idea of deterrents and the protection of society. Execution removes dangerous individuals who would otherwise be a threat to prison warders, other prisoners and – if the malefactor escapes or is prematurely released – the general public. Moreover, the threat of death is society's main weapon that can be used to deter wrongdoers; abdication of this power self-evidently leaves society more vulnerable.

The arguments against capital punishment are just as forceful. Mistakes can be made by juries. Statistical evidence has shown that states who regular-ly enforce the death penalty often have equal or greater crime problems than those that settle for imprisonment. Therefore some people question whether there is any "deterrent effect" at all.

Psychological studies of criminals, like the FBI's ViCAP (Violent Criminal Apprehension Program) show that most serious criminals rarely think about the consequences of their crimes – either to their victims or to themselves. This is, in fact, a major reason why they are criminals in the first place. The deter-rent of capital punishment seems only to deter normal, forward-thinking citizens … who are highly unlikely to indulge in capital crimes anyway.

Peter Manual, 1958

Between 1956 and 1958, Peter Manual killed seven (or more probably eight) people in and around Glasgow. Six victims were callously shot during two burglaries, while the other one (probably two) were killed as part of Manual's sexual fetishism.

Manual's sex victims were thought to be Anne Kneilands (although this remains unproved – Manual confessed to her murder then retracted the confession) and Isabelle Cook. Both young women were beaten to death, apparently so that their attacker could steal their panties.

Marion Watt, her daughter Vivienne Watt and Marion's sister Margaret Brown were ruthlessly shot by Manual during a burglary, as were Peter Smart, Doris Smart and their young son Michael during a later burglary.

Peter Manual was hanged on 11 July 1958.

Cheryl Crane, 1958

Fourteen-year-old Cheryl Crane, daughter of movie star Lana Turner, on trial for the murder of gangster Johnny Stompanato.

Turner and Stompanato had been lovers. Cheryl admitted to stabbing Stompanato in the belly with a kitchen knife when she heard him violently arguing with her mother.

The jury passed a sentence of "justifiable homicide".

Nazi Forged Fivers, 1959

During the Second World War, the Nazis forged tens of thousands of British five-pound notes – ironically using Jewish craftsmen in concentration camps to do the work. The idea of the plan was to dump the fake fivers out of bombers over Britain like confetti. The naturally dishonest British public would, the Nazis believed, pocket the forged money and the resulting inflation of the pound sterling would undermine the British war effort.

The plot got as far as dropping an experimental "bomb" full of fake notes into southern England. However, the container failed to scatter the money and was a found in a field by a farmer. He conscientiously handed it in at the local police station.

When the Germans realized that they were on the verge of defeat, they took the cases of faked notes and dropped them into Lake Toplitz in the Austrian mountains. Numerous diving expeditions – authorized and unauthorized – have searched Lake Toplitz since the war … not to find the now worthless fake fivers, but large amounts of Nazi gold, also said to have been dumped in the lake's icy Alpine waters. Searchers have had little success to date.

Caryl Chessman, 1960

Chessman became famous during the early 1950s for the long and often brilliant fight he put up to avoid execution for rape. He provided anti-capital punishment campaigners with an obvious case of injustice.

Chessman had spent much of his life in prisons and reformatories. In January 1948, he had only recently been paroled from California's Folsom Prison when he was arrested as a suspect in the case of the "Red Light Bandit".

This man had been approaching couples in cars, flashing a red light to make them think he was driving a police car. He then robbed the man and often abducted the woman to force her to perform oral sex. Apprehended after a car chase that ended in his stolen car being wrecked, Chessman was found guilty of 17 such offences, and sentenced to death.

On Death Row in San Quentin, he began to study law, and to argue his innocence. He wrote a book entitled *Cell 2455*, which became a bestseller, and provided him with funds to hire a team of lawyers to fight his case. This was the first of four books, which gained him the support of such celebrities as Aldous Huxley, Pablo Casals, Arthur Koestler and Billy Graham.

By the time he was eventually sent to the gas chamber in 1960, Chessman had received eight stays of execution. On 2 May 1960, a federal judge granted Chessman's lawyers a 30-minute delay to argue their case. But a digit was accidentally omitted from the phone number of the jail, and by the time the call was received by the warden of San Quentin, the cyanide pellet had already been dropped.

Caryl Chessman   343

Tom Ponzi, 1960

Legendary Italian private detective, Tom Ponzi, takes issue with the gaze of the press camera.

The A6 Murder, 1961

following spread

On 23 August 1961, a student found the body of a badly wounded woman on the A6, near Deadman's Hill in Bedfordshire, and a dead man lying nearby. The woman, Valerie Storie, had been shot several times and was paralysed; the man, Michael Gregsten, had been shot twice in the head.

Valerie told police that she and Gregsten had been sitting in the car in a cornfield at Dorney Reach when a man had tapped on the window with a gun. He forced them to drive for several hours, ordered them to stop at Deadman's Hill, shot Gregsten in the back of the head and raped and shot Valerie Storie. He had then driven off in the car.

An identikit picture was published of the wanted man, and an almanac salesman named Peter Alphon was questioned by police, when his landlady thought he was behaving suspiciously.

In a room of the Vienna Hotel, Maida Vale, where Alphon had stayed on the night of the murder, two spent bullet cases were found; they proved to be from the murder weapon. However, Alphon had stayed in Room 6 on the night of the murder, not Room 24, where the bullets were found. The man who had been staying in Room 24 had called himself James Ryan. This proved to be the alias used by a burglar named James Hanratty.

Hanratty was soon arrested in Blackpool, and charged with the A6 murder. Valerie Storie picked him out in an identity parade. He, however, claimed he was in Rhyll, North Wales at the time of the murder. In spite of support for this alibi from a Rhyll landlady, Hanratty was found guilty, and hanged on 4 April 1962.

After Hanratty's death, Peter Alphon made a confession to the murder, and Hanratty's father was prominent in a "Pardon Hanratty" campaign. But in 2001, newly discovered DNA evidence seemed to prove that Hanratty was guilty. The Pardon Hanratty campaign claims that this DNA evidence is a result of cross-contamination over the 40 years since the murder and rape took place.

Adolf Eichmann, 1961

In many ways Adolf Eichmann represented the very worst aspects of the Nazi regime: bigotry, corruption, cruelty and a bureaucratic inhumanity that simply beggars belief.

As a trusted officer in the SS, Eichmann was responsible for the removal of all Jews from Vienna, by deportation or arrest, by the end of 1938. He fulfilled the same role in Prague in 1939 – in both cases making a personal fortune from taking bribes and extorting money. But it was his central part, from 1942 to 1945, in the organization of the "Final Solution", the Nazi plan to exterminate every last Jew in occupied Europe, that has earned Eichmann the loathing of history.

Adolf Eichmann was in overall control of the identification, arrest, transportation and execution of millions of Jews: a task he seems to have viewed as a Herculean task of paperwork, rather than an unprecedented act of mass murder. It is entirely possible that without Eichmann's zealous organizing skills, the Holocaust would have claimed millions less people.

After the war, Eichmann escaped an American prison camp and went into hiding. He was helped to escape to (unofficially) Nazi-friendly Argentina in 1958 by the ODESSA – the secret SS aid organization.

Two years later, Eichmann was captured by Israeli secret agents and illegally smuggled out of the country. Despite Argentinian diplomatic complaints, Eichmann was put on trial in Israel in April 1961 (pictured receiving a medical examination in jail). He was found guilty of numerous crimes against humanity and hanged on 31 May 1962.

The Profumo Affair, 1963

Christine Keeler, the high-class London prostitute, whose liaison with War Minister John Profumo shook the British Conservative government.

A doctor called Stephen Ward was at the centre of the Profumo scandal. A man with many upper-class friends, Ward "introduced" them to young ladies of easy morals. In effect, Ward was a high-class pimp. His downfall came when he matched Christine Keeler with both Cabinet Minister John Profumo and a Russian Embassy naval attaché, Eugene Ivanov – a suspected Soviet spy.

Following the public revelation of his affair with Keeler, and her affair with Ivanov, Profumo made another fatal blunder: he lied to the House of Commons, claiming never to have had a sexual relationship with Christine Keeler. A sexual scandal might have been weathered, but being proved to have lied to the national debating chamber was, in 1963, a matter for automatic resignation for a minister.

Dr Stephen Ward, 1963

Although nobody ever proved (or seriously believed) that Christine Keeler had passed on any politically sensitive secrets learned from War Minister John Profumo to Soviet naval attaché Ivanov, the results of the scandal were far-reaching.

John Profumo, after being caught lying to the House of Commons, was forced to resign. Stephen Ward – who had introduced Keeler to Profumo and Ivanov – was tried for "procuring for the purposes of prostitution". And finally, the fall of the Conservative government at the next general election seems to have been as much a result of the scandal as it was their mishandling of the economy.

Dr Stephen Ward (pictured) was put on trial for procuring prostitutes and living off the their immoral earnings, and abandoned by all his important, upper-class friends. Ward killed himself on 31 July 1963, before the end of the trial.

The Krays, 1963

London gangsters, the Kray twins (centre), wine and dine Christine Keeler at the height of the Profumo Scandal.

Ronnie and Reggie Kray carefully maintained a public image as nice, well-dressed businessmen. Celebrities flocked to their nightclubs and revelled in the generous hospitality of the pair. Nevertheless, behind the scenes, the twins maintained an East End crime empire of shocking brutality.

By the mid-1960s, the Krays were beginning to overreach themselves in their gangland violence. In 1966, Ronnie shot rival gangster George Cornell dead in the Blind Beggar pub. No witnesses dared to come forward, though, and charges were dropped ... for the time being.

Thereafter, the Krays seemed to have believed they were immune to the law, thinking that nobody would dare give evidence against them. They were wrong. Following an exhaustive investigation by Detective Superintendent "Nipper" Read, they were tried and convicted for the murders of rival mobsters George Cornell, Jack "the Hat" Mcvitie and Frank "Mad Axeman" Mitchell.

They were sentenced to life imprisonment in 1969. Ronnie was later found to be criminally insane and died in the Broadmoor high-security mental hospital in 1995. Reggie was granted compassionate leave in August 2000 when he was diagnosed with bowel cancer. He died 35 days later.

The Great Train Robbery, 1963

Police investigate the site of the Great Train Robbery.

On the night of 7–8 August 1963, the mail train was travelling south towards London, carrying sacks filled with paper money – about 3 million pounds. At Sears Crossing, in Bedfordshire, the driver Jack Mills halted at a red light. His cab quickly filled with men in balaclavas, one of whom coshed him over the head as he struggled. A robber who was intended to drive the train was baffled by the new control design, however, so the befuddled Mills was ordered to drive the engine and two carriages to Bridego Bridge. There, the postal workers were overpowered and the bags of money were thrown into a lorry, which sped away.

Five days later, a massive police search finally uncovered the gang's hide-out at Leatherslade Farm, 20 miles away, but the birds had flown. However, although most surfaces had been wiped clean, enough fingerprints had been left to identify several London "villains", including jewel thief Bruce Reynolds, the organizer of the robbery.

In Bournemouth, two men trying to pay for a lockup garage with a huge wad of notes excited suspicion, and the police arrested Roger Cordrey and Gerald Boale. Ten other men were soon arrested, among them Ronald Biggs, a petty thief who had been co-opted into the gang because he knew a train driver. Bruce Reynolds had escaped abroad.

The trial opened on 20 January 1964, and in late March, savage sentences were handed down – 30 years for many, including Biggs. Even Cordrey, who had helped the police, received 20 years. Most liberal papers were shocked, the *Daily Herald* calculating that the robbers would have received less for a combination of manslaughter, blackmail and breaking a baby's arm. Reynold received 15–25 years on his eventual capture, but served only nine.

Testifying Against the Mob, 1963

Joseph Valachi informs on his former Mafia colleagues on 1 October 1963.

Mafia boss-of-bosses, Don Vitone, had ordered Valachi killed because he – mistakenly – believed he was a stool pigeon (a police informer). Valachi, already in jail, panicked when he heard the news and murdered another prisoner who he believed was his designated assassin. He then threw himself on the protection of the US authorities in return for detailed testimony of crimes of the American Cosa Nostra (an Italian name for the Mafia – obscurely meaning "our thing").

State Attorney Bobby Kennedy described Valachi's testimony as "the biggest single intelligence breakthrough yet in combatting organized crime and racketeering in the United States".

Joseph Valachi   359

The JFK Assassination, 1963

On 22 November 1963, US President John F. Kennedy was shot as his motorcade passed through Dealey Plaza, in downtown Dallas.

Kennedy, although highly popular with the nation as a whole (after averting nuclear war during the Cuban Missile Crisis) had powerful enemies nonetheless. Right-wingers did not like his "soft on Commies" political stance, the Mafia resented his crackdown on their rackets, the military resented his refusal to let them invade Cuba and even the CIA disliked his recent orders to cut their staff and halt all illegal activities not directly sanctioned by the White House.

In Dealey Plaza, President Kennedy suffered fatal rifle wounds to his neck and head, and was dead on his arrival at hospital. His corpse was immediately flown to Washington for an official autopsy. However, on arrival, it was found that some unknown person had surgically removed Kennedy's brain (presumably on the flight, as the body had not been tampered with before it left Dallas).

This ghoulish theft meant that a key piece of evidence was unavailable to investigators. If doctors had been able to examine the wounds to Kennedy's brain, they would have been able to state conclusively where the fatal bullet had been fired from – from in front of the president or from behind him.

The Warren Report – the US government investigation into Kennedy's assassination – concluded that a lone gunman, Lee Harvey Oswald, was solely responsible for the murder, firing from a school-book depot situated behind the motorcade.

Few people wholly subscribe to this view today. Much circumstantial evidence has come to light over the intervening years, which seems to point to a murderous conspiracy, possibly by forces within Kennedy's own government.

The Lee Harvey Oswald Murder, 1963

Lee Harvey Oswald – the man arrested for the assassination of President John F. Kennedy – at the moment of being shot dead outside the Dallas Police Station. Oswald had once briefly defected to Russia and also claimed to be a communist. However, there is some evidence to suggest that he was actually an undercover agent for US Intelligence.

Following his arrest, Lee Harvey Oswald was questioned for several hours by police detectives. He is said to have given a detailed statement of his innocence during this time but, against all Dallas policing regulations at that time, no record of the interview was made.

On 24 November 1963, nightclub owner and small-time hoodlum, Jack Ruby, shot and killed Oswald as the accused assassin was being transferred from Dallas police station. Oswald's last words – recorded by pressmen moments before his shooting – were: "I'm a patsy!"

The word "patsy" is underworld slang for an innocent dupe, set up to take the blame for another person's crime.

Jack Ruby, 1964

Jack Ruby, pictured while on trial for the murder of Lee Harvey Oswald.

Ruby threatened from his jail cell that he could grievously embarrass very powerful people if he told the whole truth to Senator Warren's JFK assassination investigation committee. When a journalist asked him to clarify his statement, Ruby replied that the one who had most to lose was the very man who had ascended to the White House following the murder: Kennedy's Vice President Lyndon B. Johnson.

Before he could fulfil his threat to shake the powers-that-be, however, Ruby suddenly died of previously undiagnosed cancer.

Mississippi Burning, 1964

previous spread

When civil rights workers Andrew Goodman, James Earl Chaney and Michael Henry Schwerner disappeared one night while driving through Mississippi, the Federal authorities made a major effort to solve the mystery.

FBI investigators found that Ku Klux Klan members – some in the local police department – had murdered the young men and buried them on a local farm, where the bodies were then unearthed.

Having at first been resentful, even violent, in the face of the Federal intervention, many white Mississippians were horrified by the evidence of Klan corruption and brutality uncovered by the FBI investigation.

Ronnie Biggs Toasts His Escape, 1965

In 1965, Ronald Biggs and three other Great Train Robbers escaped from Wandsworth Prison by going over the wall, through the roof of a waiting furniture van on to mattresses, then into getaway cars and away.

The fellow prisoner who arranged the escape, Paul Seabourne, received an additional four years to his sentence for his part in the escape.

Biggs had plastic surgery and fled to Australia, where his wife Charmian joined him in hiding (pictured). But after four years, dental x-rays revealed his identity. Biggs swiftly moved to Rio de Janeiro, and impregnated a 19-year-old stripper, which meant that he could not be extradited under Brazilian law. He went on to become Britain's most famous criminal exile. But after three strokes (the last of which struck him dumb) and a shortage of cash, he decided to return to England in 2001 for medical treatment, and was immediately returned to jail.

5 THE AGE OF SERIAL KILLERS

The final decades of the 20th century witnessed the increasing role of terrorism – the Baader-Meinhof gang in Germany, the Red Brigade in Italy, the Japanese Red Army. But above all, they carried the stamp of the serial killer.

It was Henry Lee Lucas to whom Ressler's term "serial killer" was most frequently applied. Born in 1937, the son of a prostitute, he was treated sadistically as a child, but was taught by one of his mother's lovers to stab sheep while committing bestiality. In January 1960 he murdered his mother in the course of a quarrel and received a sentence of 40 years. Paroled after ten years in spite of his protests (he liked the security of prison), he raped and killed a woman on the day of his release. In Florida he became the lover of a vagrant named Ottis Toole, and also of his nine-year-old sister Becky. He and Toole then took Becky and her younger brother Frank with them on a tour around the country, during which Lucas and Toole committed dozens of murders – Becky even helped bury the bodies. When Becky was caught and sent to a juvenile detention centre, Lucas and Toole helped her escape, and they went on another killing spree. Lucas later claimed a total of 360 victims, but most police investigators reject this figure, convinced that Lucas was simply seeking notoriety as America's most prolific killer. (He may, even so, have gained that status, since 157 of his murders have been confirmed.) Lucas later murdered Becky as well.

In prison on suspicion of another murder, Lucas decided to confess, and America was staggered; he made Americans aware of the number of "mobile" serial killers in their midst. Sentenced to death several times, Lucas is still, at the time of writing, in prison, now looking much fatter and more contented than in early photographs.

Another sensational case was the mass murders committed by Jeffrey Dahmer, Milwaukee's "cannibal killer", who murdered 17 males and often ate parts of their bodies. On 22 July 1991, a police patrol car was waved down by a young black man wearing handcuffs, who said that a white man had threatened to kill him and eat his heart. He led them to an apartment block, and the door was opened by a tall, good-looking young man who seemed so calm that the police assumed this was a false alarm – until they noticed the odour of decaying flesh. In a plastic bag in the kitchen they found a human head; they also found five skulls and three male torsos. At the police station, 31-year-old Dahmer admitted that he had been killing and eating for years – ever since, at the age of 18, he had invited a hitchhiker home for drinks then bludgeoned him to death when he wanted to leave.

At the trial, relatives of the victims screamed and raged at Dahmer, who expressed his remorse at what had happened, and asked forgiveness. He was sentenced to life imprisonment in February 1993. He was killed in jail by a fellow prisoner, hit on the head with an iron bar, in November 1994.

After his sentence, Dahmer made the interesting remark: "I couldn't find any meaning in my life when I was out there – I'm sure as hell not going to find it in here". It is a comment that seems to apply to all serial killers: they kill out of a kind of tunnel vision, a feeling that life has no meaning. With rare exceptions, they are motivated by sex – killing in an attempt to find a flash of meaning, like striking a match in the dark. When it goes out, they strike another.

Equally bizarre and terrifying has been the new phenomenon of "crazy gunmen" who kill at random. In a case at Columbine High School at Littleton, Colorado, two disaffected teenagers shot and killed 12 fellow students and a teacher and injured 40 more; the killers then turned their guns on themselves.

Search of the Moors, 1965

Lesley Ann Downey's mother, Mrs Ann Downey, watches the police search on Saddleworth Moor, outside Manchester, on 18 October 1965. Four days later, on October 22, Lesley's body was found.

Ten-year-old Lesley Ann Downey was the fourth victim of the Moors Murderers – Ian Brady and Myra Hindley. The first three victims had been: Pauline Reade, 16, on 12 July 1963; John Kilbride, 12, on 23 November 1963; and Keith Bennett, 12, on 16 June 1964.

On 26 December 1964, Lesley was picked up, like the earlier victims, by Myra Hindley. She was taken back to the house in Wardle Brook Avenue, that Hindley and Brady shared with Myra's grandmother, and made to undress, after which Brady took pictures of her. Her pleas to be allowed to return home were tape-recorded. Then she was raped by Brady, and strangled – Brady claims – by Hindley.

The fifth and final victim, Edward Evans, was a 17-year-old homosexual who was picked up by Brady on 6 October 1964, and was taken back to Wardle Brook Avenue.

Towards midnight, Hindley called at the home of her sister Maureen, and asked Maureen's husband, David Smith, to walk her home. Smith, 17, was an admirer and disciple of the charismatic Brady. A few minutes after they arrived, Hindley shouted "Dave, help him!" Smith ran into the sitting room to find Brady killing Evans with an axe.

After the murder, Smith was asked to help carry the body upstairs. Later, when Smith arrived home, he vomited and told his wife what had happened; she told him to go to the police. Brady and Hindley were arrested early the next morning.

The Moors Murders, 1965

following spread

Ghoulish souvenir photographs, taken on Saddleworth Moor by Ian Brady and Myra Hindley after burying their victims, led police to the shallow graves of Lesley Ann Downey and John Kilbride.

Myra Hindley, 1965

Born in Manchester in 1942, Myra Hindley (pictured) met Ian Brady in January 1961, when she went to work as a typist at Millwards Merchandising, where Ian Brady was a stock clerk. She became heavily infatuated and allowed Brady to seduce her early in 1962. A manipulative admirer of Hitler and the Marquis de Sade, Brady was soon moulding her mind like wax.

Ian Brady, 1965

Brady in the back of a police car, on the day after Lesley Ann Downey's shallow grave was discovered on Saddleworth Moor. He continued to insist that the murder of Edward Evans had been in self-defence, and that Lesley Ann Downey had been brought to the house in Wardle Brook Avenue by two men, who had taken her away after taking the photographs.

Brady, born in Glasgow in 1938, became a burglar as a child. Sent to Manchester to join his mother as a teenager, he was sentenced to four years in prison for helping a friend load some stolen lead. A sense of injustice filled him with a desire for revenge on society.

Just as in the Leopold and Loeb case, 21 years before, Brady believed his (self-defined) intellectual superiority to his fellow citizens put him morally above their petty laws. But where Leopold and Loeb had murdered to prove their own superiority to the common herd, Brady murdered as an act of self-gratifying revenge. The world had made him suffer, he believed, so the world was going to pay.

On 19 April 1966, Brady and Hindley appeared at the Chester Assizes. The tape, made by Brady, of Lesley Ann Downey's pathetic pleas for mercy was played in court and shocked the nation.

On 6 May 1966, both Brady and Hindley were sentenced to life imprisonment (the death penalty had been abolished the previous year).

The Boston Strangler, 1967

Between June 1962 and January 1964, Albert DeSalvo raped and strangled 13 women in the city of Boston, Massachusetts.

As a serial killer, DeSalvo showed several unusual traits: he started to feel pity for his victims and eventually managed to cure himself of the urge to murder (although not the urge to rape) and he actually confessed rather than being caught by the police. Such signs of humanity are rare, if not altogether unknown, in serial crime cases but, despite these mitigating circumstances, DeSalvo remained a monster by anyone's standards.

Initially targeting elderly ladies, DeSalvo talked his way into their homes, choked them unconscious, raped them, strangled them and finally would leave the corpse in an obscene position.

After four such killings, DeSalvo ceased to target old ladies and started murdering attractive young women (leading one psychiatrist to speculate that the Boston Strangler was "progressing" as a killer – having rid himself of a mother fixation, he had moved on to the serial killer's version of puberty). Fortunately, after nine more murders, DeSalvo became sickened by killing – partly through guilt, because some of his victims had been kind and friendly to him before he attacked them.

He continued to talk his way into homes to rape women, however – 200 between January and October 1964, he later claimed. Arrested for rape and sent to a mental institution, DeSalvo confessed to being the Boston Strangler. At first nobody believed him, but the exact details of the crimes he gave eventually convinced the authorities that they had accidentally caught the man who had kept the entire city under a pall of fear for almost three years.

DeSalvo was stabbed to death in his cell in 1973. His murderer, presumably another prisoner, has never been identified.

The Mafia on Trial, 1967

Accused Mafia men stand on trial in Catanzaro, Italy in 1967. They were caged in the courtroom to prevent escape attempts.

The Mafia, originating in Sicily in the Middle Ages, was originally a secret movement dedicated to ousting the various invaders – like the Normans, Spaniards and Arabs – who used the island as a staging post to attack other parts of the Mediterranean. From this laudable beginning, the Sicilian Mafia deteriorated over the centuries into the ruthless crime organization it is today.

Attempts have been made throughout the 20th century to break the Mafia's power in Sicily and Southern Italy – with numerous trials and convictions of Mafia thugs and bosses.

Unfortunately the Sicilian/Italian Mafia always has plenty of new recruits and makes more than enough money to weather such attacks. Moreover, the Mafia retaliates by either bribing officials or, when they cannot be corrupted, murdering them.

The MLK Assassination, 1968

On the morning of 4 April 1968, civil rights leader, Dr Martin Luther King, was shot dead by a sniper while standing on the balcony of the Lorraine Hotel in Memphis, Tennessee.

Small-time criminal James Earl Ray was caught, confessed and was convicted of Dr King's assassination, receiving a 99-year sentence. Ray later claimed he was actually innocent and that his confession had been tricked out of him, on the promise of a lenient sentence. Some researchers believe that he was yet another assassination "patsy" – an innocent framed to protect the real murderer(s).

The collar of Dr King's shirt shows where the rifle bullet passed. The shot blew a large hole in the right side of Dr King's face, but he nevertheless took several hours to die. The shirt, on a cursory inspection, might seem to back Ray's story.

Ray was supposed to have fired from a motel bathroom window, some distance away and slightly above the balcony on which Dr King was standing. The bullet hole in the shirt collar suggests the short was fired from below, and therefore fairly near to the assassination scene.

The RFK Assassination, 1968
the following spread

On the evening of 5 June 1968, Robert F. Kennedy – the great hope for the Democratic Party following the murder of his brother, President John F. Kennedy – was shot in the head, just behind the left ear, as he was being led through the kitchen of the Ambassador Hotel. Palestinian, Sirhan Bashira Sirhan was apprehended at the scene.

Despite the fact that Sirhan Sirhan, the presumed assassin, had leapt at Kennedy firing a handgun, it seems highly improbable that the Palestinian was the actual murderer. Sirhan was pulled down by onlookers over six feet from, and directly in front of, Kennedy. Yet the killing wound showed powderburns from the muzzle of the gun, proving that it must have been within six inches of him when it was fired. Whoever shot Bobby Kennedy must have been standing close behind him, and thus could not have been Sirhan. The Palestinian was, however, jailed for life for the murder.

ROW
AND WEAR
ECTOCENE
MADE IN U.S.A.

6-2 78
DATE
KING
MCL NUMBER

EVIDENCE
METROPOLITAN POLICE DEPT. WASH. D.C. 20001
CRIME SCENE EXAMINATION SECTION

Stashed Banknotes, 1968

The Great Train Robbery in 1963 netted 2.6 million pounds. Staggering as this sum was for that period, it presented its own peculiar problem: namely, how to spend the stuff without drawing attention to yourself.

Laundering (concealing the origin and ownership of stolen money through depositing it in foreign banks or investment in legitimate businesses) was not immediately possible for such a huge sum – especially for ill-educated London thugs with no financial connections. Until the authorities relaxed their vigilance, therefore, there was little choice other than "stashing the cash".

This ran its own risk, however. As the authorities were soon pretty sure who had been involved in the train robbery, they simply had to trace each robber's movements after the heist. Even so, Great Train Robbery cash was still being found years after the event.

Here, 35,000 pounds is discovered hidden in the walls of a caravan owned by Great Train Robber, James White, on 5 February 1968.

Charles Manson, 1969

The swastika Charles Manson cut into his forehead with a razor during the course of his trial.

A repeat offender from the age of nine, Charles Milles Manson was released from prison in 1967. At the age of 33, he had already spent more than half his life in jail, all for fairly minor offences. Moving to San Francisco – unofficial capital of the hippy movement – Manson found himself surrounded by a libertarian world he had never dreamed existed.

A very articulate person, despite his past, Manson quickly set himself up as a hippy guru, and soon gathered what he called his "Family" of followers – all young, white and middle-class. Group sex and drug taking were key parts of the Manson message.

Manson also taught the Family that a race war, followed by a nuclear war, would destroy civilization – his name for this apocalypse was "Helter Skelter" – a term lifted from a Beatles song.

In 1969, Manson decided to get the apocalyptic ball rolling by murdering prominent whites, and leaving false evidence that black extremists had committed the crimes.

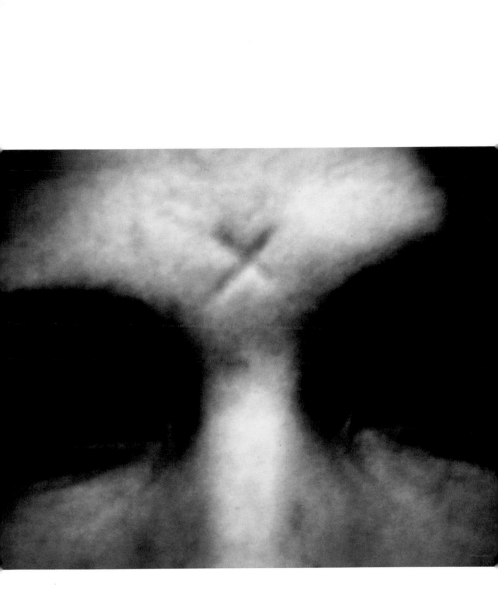

The Manson "Family" Murders, 1969

In all, members of Manson's Family (pictured) killed eight people – including actress Sharon Tate, wife of director Roman Polanski, who was stabbed in the stomach while eight months pregnant.

Manson himself merely ordered the murders, choosing not even to be present when they took place. Manson's remote-controlled killers were Susan Atkins, Tex Watson, Bobby Beausoleil, Bruce Davis, Patricia Krenwinkel, Leslie van Houton and Clem Grogan. Mary Brunner and Linda Kasabian acted as lookouts during the murders, but later gave evidence against the others, and thus escaped prosecution. These nine, Manson and 11 other members of the Family were arrested less than a week after their last murder.

Manson and seven Family members received the death sentence for the eight murders, but these were all commuted to life-imprisonment when California chose to abolish the death penalty in 1972. Manson, despite one failed attempt to escape with a mail-order hot-air balloon, has remained in jail ever since.

Teddy Kennedy's Car Crash, 1969
following spread

Senator Edward Kennedy's car is pulled from the water.

On 19 July 1969, Teddy Kennnedy crashed this car through the barrier of a bridge at Chappaquidick Island, Massachusetts, on the road leading to Martha's Vineyard.

Teddy Kennedy was the younger brother of John and Bobby Kennedy, both previously assassinated. He survived the crash but his companion, 28-year-old Mary Jo Kopechne, was drowned. Kennedy was later convicted of leaving the scene of an accident.

K EM! WE FETCH EM!

The Mafia Good Life, 1971

Italian Mafiosi dining on the island of Linosa, near Agrigento, on the south coast of Sicily. They are (from left to right): Vincenzo Parlpiano (of the Agrigento Mafia), Salvatore Sanfilippo (Agrigento), Rosario de Maggio (of the Palermo Mafia), Calogero Migliore (Agrigento), Damiano Cumella (Vallone Mafia) and Rosario Mancino (Palermo).

Soon after this photograph was taken, all of them were arrested.

Mob Rights, 1971
following spread

To try to combat the general perception that the American Mafia was run by Italians (and that all American Italians were in the Mafia) Joe Colombo, head of a New York crime family, conceived the idea of the Italian-American Civil Rights League.

Colombo (carrying the sign) had come to power as a result of an attempt by the Bonanno family to take over the New York Mafia. Colombo was ordered to kill top Mafiosi like Carlo Gambino and Tommy Lucchese, but betrayed the plot to the would-be victims, who rewarded him by making him head of the Profaci crime family.

Colombo was shot by a black gangster, Jerome A. Johnson at a rally of the Italian American League on 28 June 1971, on the orders of mobster Joey Gallo. Johnson was immediately killed by Colombo's bodyguard; Colombo survived, but was little better that a vegetable. He died seven years later.

Emperor Bokassa, 1972

previous spread

The bodies of convicted thieves lie on display, executed on the orders of President Jean-Bedel Bokassa of the Central African Republic in August 1972.

Born in the French colony of Equatorial Africa in 1921, Bokassa joined the French army and served against the Nazis in France and, after the war, against anti-French insurgents in Algeria and Indochina. When French Equatorial Africa was granted independence in 1960 (renaming itself the Central African Republic) Bokassa was invited by the CAR's new president (and his cousin) David Dacko, to head the county's armed forces.

In 1966, Bokassa overthrew Dacko in a military coup and named himself the new president. Thereafter Bokassa's rule became increasingly autocratic and brutal. In 1972 he named himself "president-for-life", and in 1977 he crowned himself Emperor Bokassa I.

In 1979, Bokassa had 100 children imprisoned for demonstrating against the cost of school uniforms, and then executed them all. Some witnesses claimed that he took part in the killings personally and later ate some of his victims.

French paratroops deposed Bokassa and reinstated Dacko as president later that same year. Ironically, Bokassa, fleeing from justice in his own country, was eventually granted asylum in France.

Inexplicably Bokassa returned to the Central African Republic in 1986, despite having been condemned to death in absentia. He was found guilty of killing the 100 children but was acquitted of cannibalism. However, he later had his death sentence commuted to 20 years' imprisonment, of which he served only seven before being released. He died in his family home in 1996.

The Olympic Massacre, 1972

A Palestinian terrorist stands on the balcony of the Munich Olympic Village during the hostage crisis of the 1972 games.

Eight Palestinian terrorists burst into the Israeli team's quarters, immediately killing two people and holding a further nine hostage. They demanded the release of 200 Palestinian prisoners held in Israeli jails, and threatened to shoot more hostages if their demands were not met.

The German police attempted a rescue, but this led to all the hostages, five of the terrorists and one policeman being killed.

Andreas Baader of the Red Army Faction, 1972

The Red Army Faction was a West German communist terror group who robbed banks, kidnapped industrialists, firebombed department stores and bombed American military bases in the 1970s – all in the name of defeating capitalism. The founding members were a mixed, if uniformly middle-class group: Horst Mahler (a socialist defence lawyer), Ulrike Meinhof (a respected left-wing journalist), Gudrun Ensslin (a philosophy student and arsonist) and her lover, Andreas Baader (a layabout with no political convictions, but a taste for fast cars, guns and adventure).

In May 1972, after training in terrorist tactics with Palestinian militants, the RAF – nicknamed the Baader-Meinhof Gang – set off a number of bombs in West Germany. Within the year, all founding members of the group had been arrested.

This led to a number of terrorist atrocities by remaining RAF members and affiliated Palestinian groups: the hijacking of two jetliners and the kidnapping of industrialist Hans-Martin Schleyer, to name but three. In each case, the release of the Baader-Meinhof leaders was demanded.

In 1975, Ulrike Meinhof apparently hanged herself in prison (or, as some believe, was raped and strangled to death). Following the failure of a hijacking in October 1977, Baader, Ensslin and another gang member, Jan-Carl Raspe, also apparently entered a suicide pact and killed themselves on the same night. A fourth RAF member, Irmgard Moller, was found alive with stab wounds in her left breast.

However, on recovery, Moller insisted that there had been no suicide pact, and that unknown persons had attacked them in their cells. Although the West German authorities stridently denied this claim, it is hard not to suspect that they secretly executed the Baader-Meinhof leaders to avoid further terrorist atrocities.

The RAF itself continued, with a much lower terror profile, until it announced its disbandment in 1992.

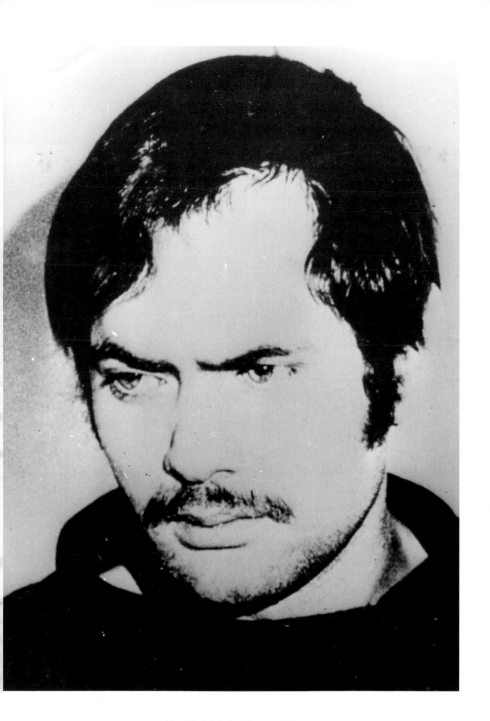

Baader-Meinhof Gang   405

The Watergate Building and President Nixon, 1972

On 17 June 1972, five men were caught breaking into the Democratic Party Headquarters, in the Watergate Building, Washington DC. This apparently petty affair was eventually to bring down incumbent Republican president, Richard Nixon (inset).

The burglars were a team of secret and illegal operatives run by Nixon and his White House staff, and nicknamed "the Plumbers" (because they were originally set up to stop information leaks).

The arrest of the Plumbers, committing a burglary to steal politically sensitive documents from the Democrats, caught the interest of journalists from the *Washington Post* newspaper. The resulting investigation and scandal eventually led to a full congressional inquiry into the Watergate break-in.

The Watergate Scandal, 1973

James McCord (pictured) spilled the beans while on trial as one of the Watergate burglars. McCord presented a letter to the presiding judge, in which he claimed that the White House had ordered the burglars to plead guilty in order to avoid revelations of presidential involvement in the break-in. The result was a full senatorial investigation into the Watergate burglary and the White House's possible involvement.

Revelations of the dirty tricks employed by the Nixon campaign team – mostly by the maverick "Plumbers", a small criminal task force, paid for out of an illegal "slush-fund" – shocked the world. All attempts at cover-up failed to hide the fact that many of the Nixon White House team were heavily involved in illegal political activities. Tapes, made by the president of every important conversation in the White House, were eventually released, but were proved to have been tampered with, apparently to remove incriminating evidence.

President Nixon could not convince the public that he was uninvolved in the illegal goings-on and resigned on 8 August 1974, rather than wait to be impeached by Congress. The new president, Republican Gerald Ford, immediately granted Nixon a full pardon.

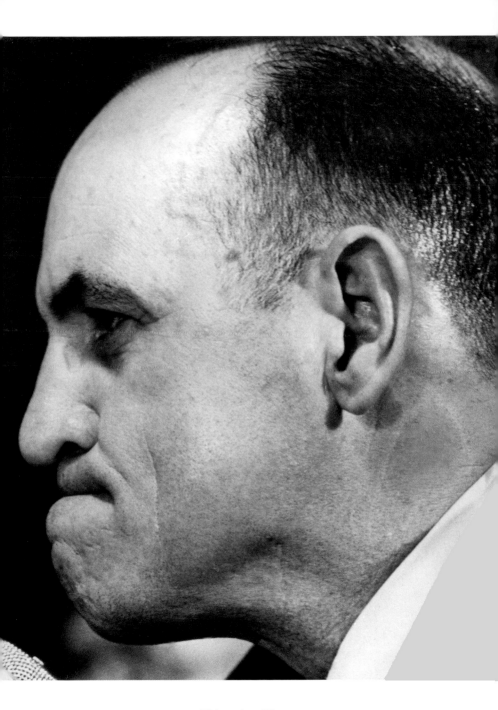

Mary Flora Bell, 1973

In 1968, an 11-year-old Newcastle schoolgirl, Mary Flora Bell, strangled two small boys to death: Martin Brown, aged four, and Brian Howe, aged three. Considered sane but emotionally unstable from her poverty-stricken and unaffectionate home life, Mary – who happily admitted, "I like hurting people" – was found guilty of manslaughter in both cases.

Mary Bell was first sent to Moor Court open prison (pictured at age 16). In 1977, on being transferred to another facility, she managed to escape with another inmate, but was recaptured after three days. Mary claimed that she had merely been trying to prove that she was safe to function out in society. This proved true when she was later released to live under an assumed name.

Mary Bell Case   411

Patty Hearst and the Symbionese Liberation Army, 1974

Millionaire heiress Patty Hearst (pictured in 1970) was kidnapped in 1974 by the American-Maoist terrorist group, the Symbionese Liberation Army.

Hearst was successfully brainwashed into joining the group and later helped them commit a bank robbery. She was filmed during the robbery by security cameras and, when recaptured in 1975, she was sentenced to seven years, despite the clear evidence that the terrorists had programmed her to help them.

Donald Nielson, The Black Panther, 1974

The Black Panther was an armed robber who terrorized post offices in England in 1974, killing three sub-post masters in the course of over a dozen raids. Then, on 14 January 1975, 17-year-old heiress Lesley Whittle was kidnapped near her home and a ransom of 50,000 pounds was demanded. In March 1975, police found Lesley Whittle's corpse, hanged with a wire rope.

Eight months later, police and members of public violently apprehended Donald Nielson (pictured) as he was about to commit another post-office robbery. Forensic evidence proved he was both the Black Panther and the kidnapper/murderer of Lesley Whittle. He received a life sentence for the murders and 61 years for the kidnapping.

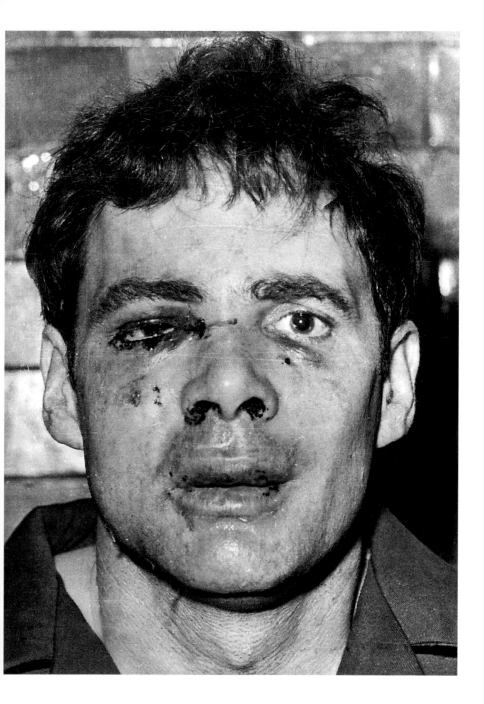

The Lord Disappears, 1974

On 7 November 1974, the nanny of Lord and Lady Lucan was found battered to death with a lead pipe in their flat in Belgravia, west London. Lord Lucan was nowhere to be found, but his bloodstained car was discovered at Newhaven in Sussex.

Lord Lucan, it was revealed, had tremendous gambling debts. It seems likely that he meant to kill Lady Lucan (pictured shortly after her husband's disappearance) for her life insurance, making it look like the work of burglars, but accidentally killed their children's nanny, Sandra Rivett, instead. Panicking, Lucan went on the run.

Lord Lucan has yet to be discovered. It is believed that he either committed suicide or successfully assumed another identity.

Damaged Safety Deposit Boxes Following a Bank Robbery, 1975
following spread

The 1970s were the last decade in which bank robbery was a lucrative criminal activity. Not just professional thieves, but political terror groups like the Symbionese Liberation Army and the Baader-Meinhof Gang robbed banks to finance their activities.

Improved security and harsh jail sentences have made bank robbery a much less common crime in the last two decades. Also, the greatly increased use of credit cards and the electronic transfer of money means that credit card fraud and computer hacking have become much safer and more lucrative methods of robbing financial institutions.

Palestinian Hijacker Leila Khaled, 1975

Palestinian hijacker Leila Khaled, known for concealing hand-grenades in her underwear, hides out with a Kalashnikov assault rifle (AK-47) in Beirut, circa 1975.

The 1970s became the decade of the plane hijacker. Many, from escaping criminals to political asylum seekers, tried to take over jet planes at gunpoint. Landless and displaced Palestinian extremists made hijacking their chief tool for making political demands.

Hijacks became much less common after many governments made it plain by their actions, in the late 1970s and early 1980s, that they would risk passengers' lives by sending heavily armed shock troops into grounded hijack planes, rather than give in to political blackmail – thus making hijackers virtually certain to end up as "martyrs for the cause".

Leila Khaled 421

The Hans-Martin Schleyer Kidnapping, 1977

Hans-Martin Schleyer, 61, was a German industrialist kidnapped in Cologne. Schleyer's car was fired upon, killing the driver. His three bodyguards, travelling in the car behind Schleyer's, were also machine-gunned to death. The kidnappers were members of the communist terror group called the Red Army Faction (RAF), better known as the Baader-Meinhof gang.

At the time, key members of the RAF including Andreas Baader were being held in prison. Another key member, Ulrike Meinhof, had already been found hanged in her cell, two years earlier. Although the authorities insisted it was suicide, apparent evidence of rape and strangulation seemed to point to murder – or an unofficial execution.

The Schleyer kidnappers demanded the immediate release of the surviving RAF members. Unfortunately, following a separate failed hijacking, where the hijackers had also demanded the release of the RAF member, Baader and two other founding members of the RAF committed suicide in their cells – or were secretly executed, depending on how one views the evidence.

In retaliation, Schleyer was executed by the RAF. His throat was slit and he was shot three times in the head.

Son of Sam, 1977

David Berkowitz – also known as "Son of Sam" – terrorized New York in the summer of 1977. He shot lone young women and couples courting in parked cars, killing seven and seriously wounding eight.

Berkowitz also wrote taunting letters to the police (signed "Son of Sam") and was eventually caught when police traced a ticket that his car had picked up when illegally parked during one of the murders.

Berkowitz proved to live in a fantasy world and claimed he had been told to kill people by his neighbour's pet Labrador dog. He received 365 years' imprisonment.

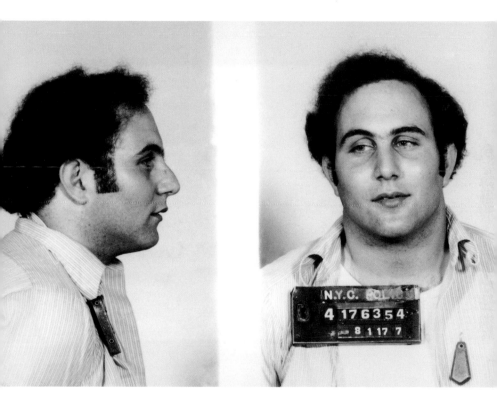

The Beauty Queen and the Mormon Missionary, 1977

One of the more bizarre cases of 1977 was that of Joyce McKinney, a Wyoming beauty queen in her late twenties who apparently had a 21-year-old Mormon missionary, Kirk Anderson, kidnapped. She had developed an unquenchable passion for him and had chased him all the way to Britain from the United States – funding her hunt with money earned as a pornographic model. Anderson insisted that he had been abducted against his will and had been chained to a bed so McKinney could force sex on him for three days.

Under arrest, McKinney held up a sign to pressmen, saying: "Kirk left with me <u>willingly</u>! He fears excommunication for leaving his mission and made up this kidnap-rape story." Uncertain if this defence would stick, however, McKinney and her male accomplice skipped bail and returned to the United States. Although sentenced, in absentia, to a year in prison, extradition for Joyce McKinney was never applied for.

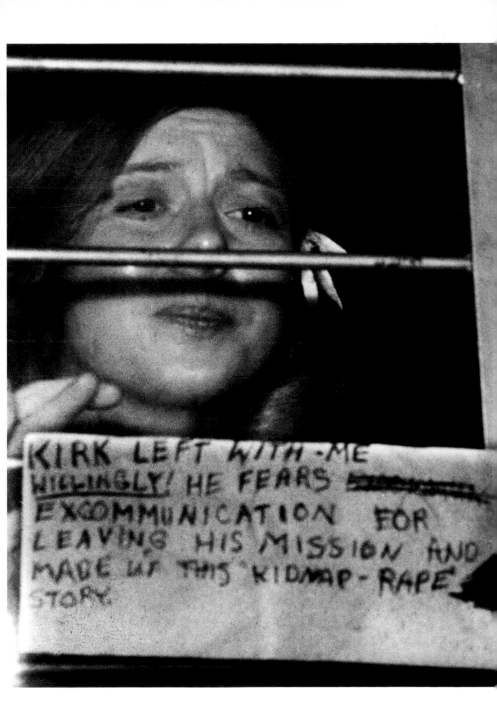

KIRK LEFT WITH ME
WILLINGLY! HE FEARS
EXCOMMUNICATION FOR
LEAVING HIS MISSION AND
MADE UP THIS "KIDNAP-RAPE"
STORY.

Acid Stash, 1978

The sitting room of a house in Tregaron, Wales, shortly after police found a large haul of illegal Lysergic Acid Diethylamide (LSD – also known as "acid") buried under the floor.

LSD is a powerful hallucinogenic, synthesized, under laboratory procedures, to mimic ergot alkaloids. Such alkaloids block serotonin production in the brain, producing "trips": short-term dream- (or nightmare-) like states, similar to those suffered by schizophrenics.

Undesirable as this may sound, the effect of LSD has been compared to the ecstasies sometimes enjoyed by religious believers. Indeed, an experiment carried out by the American Catholic Church in 1965 (involving two batches of seminary students – one using fervent prayer to achieve Divine bliss, the others on LSD) found that the religious visions seen under the drug could not be disallowed as possibly true revelations from God. However, the report was quickly suppressed. The libertarian Hippy movement in the US and Europe had greatly taken to LSD, and most governments had, by then, banned it except for use in scientific and mental institutions.

The press have published many scare stories about LSD (the usual one being about a user – convinced that he or she could fly – falling to their death) but there is little actual proof that the drug constitutes a major danger to cautious users. It is not addictive and, unlike alcohol, LSD does not make users violent or otherwise reckless of physical dangers.

Indeed, an exhaustive test carried out by the US Government in the early 1980s found, much to their irritation, that LSD actually increases the IQ of first-time users by up to ten percent for a short time. On the other hand, habitual users, or those already suffering a mental imbalance, risk serious psychological breakdown through the use of LSD. They can become so-called "acid-casualties".

Acid continues to be illegally smuggled in industrial nations, but never in as large amounts as drugs like heroin, ecstasy and hashish.

The Thorpe Case, 1978

The British Liberal Party leader, Jeremy Thorpe (pictured) was considered one of the more brilliant politicians of his generation. Becoming leader of his party in 1967, at the youthful age (for British politics) of 37, many believed that he had the potential to be the first Liberal Prime Minister in half a century.

Unfortunately, Thorpe was also dogged by rumours of closet homosexuality – especially due to his ambiguous relationship with a male model called Norman Josiffe, who later to change his surname to Scott.

Scott was self-obsessed, emotionally disturbed and also seems to have been a habitual liar, so it was hardly surprising that he was virtually blackmailing Thorpe by 1970. When Thorpe refused to help him financially, Scott went to the newspapers, claiming that Thorpe had shamefully wronged him – seducing him in 1960, then cruelly abandoning him and refusing to help with his many financial difficulties. The papers refused to touch the story when it turned out that Scott had no proof to back his claims.

Scott continued to be a thorn in Thorpe's side and risk to his career, however. On 24 October 1975, Scott was driven out on to Exmoor by a man called Andrew Newton, on the pretext of warning Scott about a plot to kill him formed by Jeremy Thorpe. Newton then shot Scott's dog and apparently tried to shoot Scott as well, but his gun jammed. Picked up by the police, Newton claimed that Scott had been blackmailing him and that he had shot Scott's dog to frighten him. He received two years in prison.

The following year, facing a charge of defrauding the Social Security, Scott claimed in open court that he was the victim of a harassment campaign by Thorpe because they had been lovers. The story was now inescapably public. Thorpe resigned as leader of the Liberal Party on 10 May 1976, although still proclaiming his innocence of any sexual relationship with Scott.

On his release, Newton went to the newspapers, claiming he had been paid 5,000 pounds to kill Scott by two businessmen, John Le Mesurier and George Deakin, and a friend of Jeremy Thorpe, David Holmes. Le Mesurier, Deakin, Holmes and Thorpe were tried for conspiracy to commit murder in May 1979.

All four were acquitted, partly because the evidence against them was almost entirely circumstantial, but mostly because both Scott and Newton – appearing for the prosecution – had proved to be very unprepossessing witnesses. Nevertheless, Jeremy Thorpe's political career was effectively over.

The Yorkshire Ripper, 1978

A photofit picture of the Yorkshire Ripper, a savage serial killer who terrorized the north of England from 1975 to 1978. The murderer attacked and killed 13 women, knocking them unconscious with a ball-hammer and then slashing them to death with a chisel.

The hunt for the Yorkshire Ripper was one of the largest ever undertaken by a British police force. It was wholly unsuccessful, however, due to bad luck and, more importantly, slipshod and out-of-date investigation methods.

For example, by the end of the investigation the police had collected a mountain of relevant clues, but a totally inadequate filing system made even basic cross-referencing all but impossible.

Yorkshire Ripper   433

Peter Sutcliffe, 1978

Peter Sutcliffe, the Yorkshire Ripper, is led to court under a blanket to hide his face from press photographers.

Despite the huge effort made by the police and public to apprehend the Yorkshire Ripper, Peter Sutcliffe was finally caught by accident: a policeman found him in the back of a car with a prostitute, and a search revealed that he was carrying the infamous Ripper's ball-hammer and chisel.

Sutcliffe was initially sentenced to life-imprisonment as a sane offender, but was diagnosed insane after a suicide attempt and was sent to a maximum-security hospital.

Sonia Sutcliffe, The Yorkshire Ripper's wife, later successfully sued *Private Eye* magazine for suggesting that she had been aware of her husband's murderous activities.

The Jonestown Massacre , 1978
following spread

In the late 1970s, followers of the Reverend Jim Jones followed him to Guyana to form a new Christian/socialist community. In the event, "Jonestown" quickly became a petty religious dictatorship, controlled with brainwashing and armed guards.

After a personal inspection of Jonestown by California Representative Leo Ryan on 17 November 1978, Jones panicked and had Ryan and escorting journalists shot. He then ordered his followers to drink cyanide-laced coolaid (a soft drink).

Nine hundred and thirteen died, including Jones himself and 276 children. Most of Jones' followers killed themselves voluntarily, believing they were on their way to Heaven.

Nineteen years after the Jonestown Massacre, another cult voluntarily committed suicide. On 27 March 1997, 39 members of the Heaven's Gate religious group covered themselves with purple shrouds and took poison.

They believed that this was the only way to transport themselves to an alien spaceship that was to take them to Paradise.

Frank Sinatra with (Mafia) Friends, 1978

On 18 July 1972, Frank Sinatra was subpoenaed to appear before the House Committee on Crime in Washington DC. Although advised by close friends to be "docile and low-key", Sinatra lost no time in berating the Committee for accepting "hearsay" evidence about his own Mafia business connections.

Sinatra stormed out of the hearing in indignant mood and paid a journalist to write a piece attacking the Committee (under Sinatra's name) in the *New York Times*. The Committee finally backed off, Sinatra having too many influential friends.

In 1978, Sinatra's name again made headlines in association with the Mafia. The Westchester Premier Theatre (NY) was built with mob money, but was soon near bankruptcy as the mob "skimmed" much of its profits.

Ten indictments were handed down by a New York grand jury charging that racketeers, among them Carlo Gambino, stole the assets. The prosecutor alleged that Sinatra had received 50,000 dollars "under the table". Sinatra was never charged, but headlines, and the photograph of Sinatra with mobsters like Gambino (second from left), convinced many that the allegations were true. Note how one face had to be cut from the photograph early on for legal reasons.

The Red Brigade, 1978
following spread

Political terrorism was rife in late 1970s and early 1980s Italy. The Red Brigade (Brigate Rossi), an ultra-left organization opposed to the Communist Party as well as to right-wing parties, began a reign of terror in 1977, killing about 40 eminent persons – business executives and government officials.

Renato Curcio and Maurizio Ferri, the Red Brigade founders, were captured and put on trial in Turin in early 1978.

On 16 March 1978, the Red Brigade kidnapped Aldo Moro, five times Prime Minister and leader of the Christian Democratic Party, killing five of his bodyguards in the process. Their aim was to free their leaders, on trial in Turin, but the government refused to give in, and on 8 May, Moro's bullet-riddled body was found in the back of a van in Rome (pictured).

Five years later, in 1983, Prospero Gallinari, Moro's killer, and 31 other accused terrorists were all sentenced to life in prison. This was virtually the end of the Red Brigade.

Dead Judge, 1978

Italian judge Riccardo Palma was assassinated by the Red Brigade in Rome on 14 February 1978, as he stopped to buy a newspaper.

Carlos the Jackal, 1979

Ilich Ramírez Sánchez – also known as Carlos "the Jackal" – was one of the masterminds of the terrorism of the 1970s, and now claims to have been personally responsible for the deaths of 83 people.

Essentially a terrorist co-ordinator, the Jackal was linked to several hijackings and bombings during the 1970s and also the killing of 11 Israeli athletes at the 1972 Olympics in Munich. Indeed, for a while, Carlos the Jackal was considered the "international public-enemy-number-one".

His greatest terrorist success came in 1975, when Carlos is believed to have masterminded the kidnap of 11 OPEC oil ministers – the kidnappers got away with a ransom of 20 million dollars. He is also believed to have co-ordinated the failed assassination attempt on the Shah of Iran in 1979.

Carlos was abducted to France from his hiding place in Sudan in 1994. He was sentenced to life imprisonment in 1997 for masterminding a bombing in France.

The Killing Fields, 1979

following spread

The Communist Party of Cambodia, also known as the Khmer Rouge, won power from a right-wing military government in 1975, after five years of bloody civil war. If the tired people of Cambodia hoped for a period of peace and rest, they were to be disappointed.

The Khmer Rouge – under its fanatical leader, Pol Pot – instituted social and agricultural reforms that ravaged the country. In their extreme Marxist philosophy, only the peasants and uneducated workers were to be trusted. The rich, the middle class, the skilled workers and the intellectuals of Cambodia were all potential counter-revolutionaries in the eyes of Pol Pot and his followers. They were systematically arrested, tortured and – those that survived – were forcibly "re-educated" as agricultural labourers.

Forced to work and live in total squalor, often denied any tools other than their bare hands, thousands were executed on the slightest pretext or simply lay down and died in what became known as "the Killing Fields".

It is estimated that over 1.5 million people were slaughtered in this way, before the Khmer Rouge were ousted in 1979 by an invading Vietnamese army. Cambodia's skilled and intellectual classes were almost totally destroyed by less than four years of Pol Pot's repression.

Carlos the Jackal   445

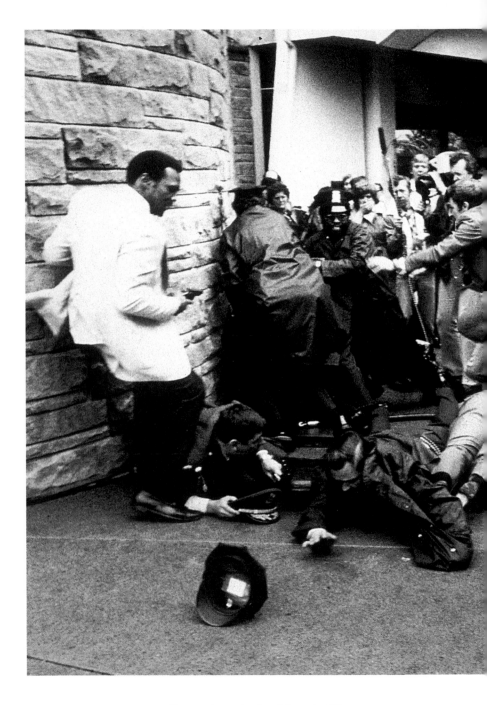

The Attempted Assassination of Ronald Reagan, 1981

previous spread

On 30 March 1981, deranged gunman John F. Hinckley Junior shot President Reagan with a handgun as the president was entering a limousine outside the Washington DC Hilton Hotel. Reagan's wound was not fatal and bodyguards disarmed Hinckley.

There was later some embarrassment when it was discovered that John Hinckley Senior (the would-be assassin's father) was an old friend of then Vice President, George Bush – Reagan's automatic successor if the shooting had proved fatal.

The Pope is Shot, 1981

On 13 May 1981, Pope John Paul II was shot and wounded in St Peter's Square, Rome. Although seriously wounded he survived. Thereafter, the Pope travelled in a bulletproof "Popemobile" whenever his safety could not be fully guaranteed in a large crowd.

The would-be papal assassin was Mehmet Ali Agca. The reasons for Agca's attempt on the Pope's life have never fully been made clear, but it is believed that, as a Turkish Moslem, he was violently opposed to the Pope's aim of spreading Catholicism into Turkey.

It has also been suggested that Agca was put up to the assassination by communists from Bulgaria, angered by John Paul II's support of the anti-Soviet Solidarity movement in Poland.

Assassination of Anwar al Sadat, 1981

previous spread

Egyptian President Anwar al-Sadat was a hero to the Arab world when he launched the attack on Israel, in October 1973, which became known as the Arab-Israeli War. However, in 1978 he signed a peace treaty with Israel, and was awarded the Nobel Peace Prize that same year.

Popular as he was internationally, Sadat made deadly enemies at home by offering the olive branch to Israel. He was gunned down by Muslim militants at a military parade – ironically, to commemorate the Arab-Israeli War – on 6 October 1981.

Henry Lee Lucas, 1983

There remains some argument over whether drifter Henry Lee Lucas was the USA's most prolific serial killer, or simply a murderer who managed to bamboozle the nation's police forces totally.

Arrested in Texas in 1983, for a minor weapons offence, Lucas unexpectedly confessed to killing more than 350 people in his hobo wanderings around the country. Initial police scepticism quickly vanished when Lucas led investigators to two bodies.

Lucas said that he, with his gay lover Ottis Toole, had set off on a killing spree across the USA. Lucas claimed that although he and Toole had murdered at least 65 people together he, on his own, had killed hundreds (his confession score eventually reached over 600).

Police departments around the country sent officers to Texas to try to clear up some of their unsolved murder files and, to their delight, Lucas gave detailed confessions to hundreds of killings. It was only later discovered that the Texas authorities were allowing Lucas to read the police files before he was asked to give any details.

Lucas later gleefully admitted that he had concocted hundreds of false confessions to humiliate the police. Nevertheless, because nobody can be sure which confessions were true (apart from some nine that have been reasonably verified) some police departments have refused to re-open murder cases that have been attributed to Henry Lee Lucas – in effect allowing possibly hundreds of murderers to escape justice.

Lucas, having had his death sentence commuted by then Senator George W. Bush, died of a heart attack in jail in March 2001.

Henry Lee Lucas   455

The Night Stalker, 1985

The Night Stalker was the nickname given to a murderous burglar and rapist who terrorized Los Angeles in 1985. He would break into family homes, shoot the man of the house in the head with a .22 pistol, rape and beat the wife or girlfriend and, on some occasions, would rape male children. Sometimes he also shot his rape victims, and he would invariably demand that survivors declare their love for Satan. If he had time, the Night Stalker would also steal any valuable household items he could find. On one occasion he gouged out a woman's eyes because she refused to tell him where she kept her money.

Throughout the spring and summer of that year there were more than 20 attacks that were traceable to the same sadistic murderer. Fortunately, surviving victims gave consistent descriptions – a tall, greasy-haired Hispanic man in his twenties with bad teeth and terrible breath.

Following his last attack, the raped wife managed to note down the number plate of his getaway car. This stolen vehicle was found dumped and recovered fingerprints allowed the police to match an identity: the Night Stalker's actual name was Ricardo Leyva Ramirez.

Ramirez was out of town when his name and photograph were printed on every newspaper front page in LA. As a result he blithely wandered into a liquor store on his return, was recognized, was chased and was nearly lynched by members of the public before he could find a policeman, into whose protection he promptly surrendered himself.

Ramirez was found guilty of 13 murders, as well as 30 other major crimes such as rape and attempted murder. Asked by reporters about how he felt after the verdict, Ramirez replied: "Evil."

After the death sentence was passed, the Night Stalker commented laconically: "Big deal. Death always went with the territory. I"ll see you in Disneyland."

The War on Drugs, 1988

The "War on Drugs", first declared by the Reagan administration in the US in the mid-1980s, was quickly picked up by other industrialized nations around the world. Unfortunately this "zero-tolerance" campaign, that attempted to educate the young while imposing harsh sentences on those caught dealing or in possession of banned substances has, in the eye of most commentators, failed. Drug use and drug-related crime has rocketed in the intervening period, including the use of crack-cocaine (pictured).

More and more countries are now looking to what has been called the "Dutch Solution": legalization of some banned drugs under state supervision and control. This certainly seems to have worked on some levels – Holland has a lower percentage of drug addicts in its population than Drug War countries like Britain and the US, and also suffers less "drug-related" crime, such as burglary and prostitution by addicts to feed their habit. However, such a course of action is strongly opposed by conservative groups.

The Red Ripper, 1990

Between 1978 and 1990, Andrei Chikatilo killed and then mutilated the corpses of at least 53 women and children around Rostov in northwestern Russia. Chikatilo claimed that he had been mentally scarred by sights he saw as a child during the Nazi occupation of his native Ukraine in the Second World War. When asked why he had killed young boys as well as girls and women, he replied, "because it felt more wicked".

He was finally executed, by a single pistol shot to the back of the neck, on 14 February 1994.

Andrei Chikatilo 461

The Death of the Branch Davidians, 1993

In 1993, the US federal authorities laid siege to the compound headquarters of David Koresh after he and fellow cult members fired on their officers.

Koresh and his followers believed that he was the second coming of Christ, and that they must arm their compound at Waco, Texas, in preparation for the coming Armageddon.

After a 53-day stand-off, the FBI sent in tear-gas firing tanks to try to drive the cultists out. Within minutes a blaze had destroyed the compound and killed the 76 people inside, including many children. The authorities claimed that Koresh and the Branch Davidians had committed suicide, but many now believe that the blaze was either accidentally or deliberately set off by the FBI themselves.

Indeed some critics of the FBI's handling of the siege believe that the compound and those inside were deliberately burned to destroy evidence that the Federal authorities had fired blind into the building from helicopters hovering over the roof (thus risking a charge of child endangerment). These critics have labelled the subsequent senatorial investigation into the conduct of the siege as a government whitewash.

The James Bulger Case, 1993

Two-year-old James Bulger is abducted from a shopping centre in Bootle, Liverpool in 1993. A security camera recorded two young boys leading James away and shortly thereafter his brutally beaten corpse was found on nearby train tracks.

Police soon arrested Jon Venables and Robert Thompson – both ten-years-old. They were convicted of kidnapping and murder. An angry mob attacked the police van carrying the two boys from court.

Venables and Thompson were released from child custody – under assumed identities – in 2001, but continue to receive public death threats through letters to the media.

James Bulger Case   465

Long Island Lolita, 1993

Sixteen-year-old Amy Fisher attends the trial of her lover, middle-aged Joey Buttafuoco. Buttafuoco was convicted of statutory rape (consensual sex with a legal minor) and was sentenced to six months in jail and fined 5,000 dollars.

However, Buttafuoco gained early release from jail on compassionate grounds, after Amy Fisher shot Mrs Buttafuoco in the face and back in revenge for reporting her affair with Joey to the authorities. The newspapers dubbed Fisher "the Long Island Lolita".

Mary-Jo Buttafuoco survived and went back to live with her husband. Amy Fisher served seven years in jail for attempted murder.

Long Island Lolita Case   467

The Bobbitt Case, 1994

Dr James Sehn displays a photograph of John Wayne Bobbitt's severed penis at Lorena Bobbitt's trial for attempted murder.

Lorena, Bobbitt's wife, cut his penis off while he was asleep and, leaving him bleeding profusely, drove away in her car. She threw the severed penis out of the car window where, fortunately, it was found by the side of the road, and later successfully reattached by surgeons.

Lorena Bobbitt was found not guilty of attempted murder, on the grounds that she had been temporally deranged due to the fact that her husband had regularly beaten her.

In a separate trial, John Wayne Bobbitt was found not guilty of abusing his wife.

The result was that Lorena was found not guilty of murderously cutting off John's penis because of beatings that another court ruled had not happened. The Bobbitts were later reported to be considering rebuilding their marriage.

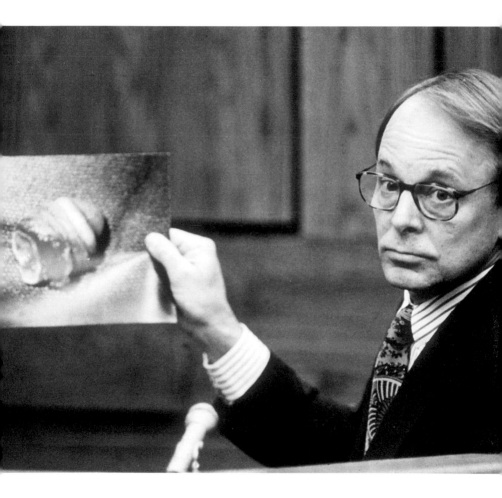

Painting by a Serial Killer, 1994

Chicago building contractor John Wayne Gacy was a respected family man who was kind-hearted enough to visit local children's wards regularly, dressed as Pogo the Clown. He was also a ruthless serial killer who, between 1972 and 1978, kidnapped, raped and murdered 33 young men and boys.

After the disappearance of a youth to whom Gacy had offered a job, investigating officers noticed an odd smell in Gacy's home. They found the bodies buried in the crawl space beneath the floor of the house.

Gacy confessed that he would go cruising for boys in his car, usually posing as a police officer. Having got a victim into his car he would chloroform him, drive him back to his house, rape him and then strangle him to death.

Gacy was originally sentenced to life imprisonment in 1980, but this was later changed to the death penalty when psychiatrists reported that his personality disorder did not amount to criminal insanity. He was not executed, however, until 1994.

The pictures Gacy had painted in jail were burned by his relatives in a public ceremony (pictured) soon afterwards.

The Murderous Marriage, 1994

In 1994 it was discovered that builder Fred West and his wife Rosemary were serial killers. Police unearthed the remains of ten girls and women from the garden and floors of 25 Cromwell Street, Gloucester, in west England.

Fred West confessed to 12 sex murders (including one of his own daughters). Rosemary West was implicated in ten of the killings and seems to have instigated many of them. It is suspected that Fred may have killed more women, but this cannot now be confirmed.

Fred West hanged himself in jail on New Year's Day, 1995, before he could be tried. Rosemary West was sentenced to ten life sentences the following November.

The building at 25 Cromwell Street, where Fred and Rosemary West raped, tortured, murdered and buried the dismembered bodies of ten women and girls, was levelled by the local council on 11 October 1996.

The Murder of Nicole Brown Simpson, 1994

Just after midnight, 13 June 1994, Nicole Brown Simpson, 35 – the estranged wife of football and movie star, Orenthal James "O.J." Simpson – was found brutally stabbed to death together with Ronald Goldman, 25, on the doorstep of her Santa Monica home. They had been murdered at around 10pm. (Goldman was a waiter at a local restaurant, and also a friend of Nicole's, who had gone to her house to return a pair of sunglasses she had left behind after dining.)

O.J. Simpson was in Santa Monica at the time of the murder, but caught a flight to Chicago at 11:45pm – less than two hours after the killings. A limousine, booked to take him to the airport had arrived at 10:25pm, but found that apparently nobody was at home. At 10:56pm the driver saw an unidentifiable man enter Simpson's home, after which Simpson emerged, claiming to have overslept.

When the police phoned Simpson, in his Chicago hotel, to tell him that his wife had been murdered, they noted that he did not ask how, when or where – the usual questions immediately asked by a relative of a murder victim. Simpson later claimed to have crushed a glass, cutting his hand, in his grief. The prosecution at his later trial claimed that this injury had actually been sustained during the murders.

The Los Angeles police treated Simpson with kid gloves; although the chief suspect, he was also a popular celebrity and had many friends in the LAPD. They even allowed him to remain free, until after Nicole's funeral, before asking him to hand himself in for arrest. This proved a mistake as Simpson failed to turn up. He was soon spotted, however, being driven by a friend in a white Ford Bronco.

There followed a farcical "slow-motion" chase in which dozens of police cars and several news helicopters followed the slow moving Bronco as it drove around the Los Angeles road system. Simpson eventually had himself driven to his home, where he was finally arrested. The car was found to contain a gun, 8,750 dollars, a passport and a false beard.

O.J. Simpson on Trial, 1995

After Nicole Simpson and her friend, Ronald Goldman, were found dead in Santa Monica, suspicions quickly fell on O.J. Simpson.

A 133-day "trial of the century" followed, with record media coverage.

The prosecution sought to show that Simpson was a jealous and abusive husband who would have preferred to murder his estranged wife rather than see her with another man. Their chief evidence for their theory – aside from numerous witnesses who had seen or heard O.J. threatening Nicole at one time or another – was the cut on Simpson's hand apparently dating from the night of the murder, and a pair of socks and a pair of leather gloves found in O.J. Simpson's home. These were stained with blood that DNA testing showed to belong almost certainly to Nicole Simpson.

The defence – dubbed the Dream Team by the press, because they comprised some of the best lawyers in the country – sought to sow a seed of doubt in the mind of the jury in the face of such apparently damning evidence. The police officer who had found the bloodied gloves, Mark Fuhrman, was asked if he ever used the "n-word" (nigger). He replied that he never did. Tapes were later played to the court of Fuhrman using the "n-word" with racist abandon, proving him to be a liar. Also on the tapes – made while he was acting as an adviser for a TV show about the LAPD – Fuhrman admitted to planting evidence to secure convictions.

Another key defence victory came when the prosecution asked Simpson to try on the gloves (pictured). They were self-evidently too small for him. Evidence only came out later that the leather gloves might well have shrunk when the blood they were coated in had dried.

The damage had been done, however. Johnnie Cochran, the chief defence lawyer, told the jury: "If it doesn't fit, you must acquit", which is exactly what they did.

The killer of Nicole Simpson and Ronald Goldman has yet to be convicted and, given that a person can't be tried twice for the same crime, many people believe the murderer has escaped justice.

The Oklahoma Bomber, 1995

On 19 April 1995 – on the second anniversary of the federal raid that led to the destruction of David Koresh's Branch Davidian cult – a bomb, hidden in a parked truck, demolished much of the Alfred P. Murrah Federal Building in Oklahoma City. One hundred and sixty-eight people, including 19 children in a crèche on the ground floor, were killed.

(Some people have suggested that the terrorist bomb was not the only cause of the disaster. Witnesses claimed to have heard a secondary explosion after the first and some believe that an armoury, maintained illegally in the public building by the federal authorities, might have been caused to explode by the eruption of the bomb.)

One British newspaper echoed the suspicions of many in the immediate aftermath of the Oklahoma bombing, printing a picture of the shattered building under the headline: "IN THE NAME OF ALLAH". The suggestion was that Islamic terrorists had been responsible. It came as something of a shock to many, therefore, when investigators arrested American Gulf War veteran, Timothy McVeigh (pictured).

McVeigh confessed to the bombing, citing his violent opposition to federal gun-control laws as his motive. He was executed on 11 June 2001.

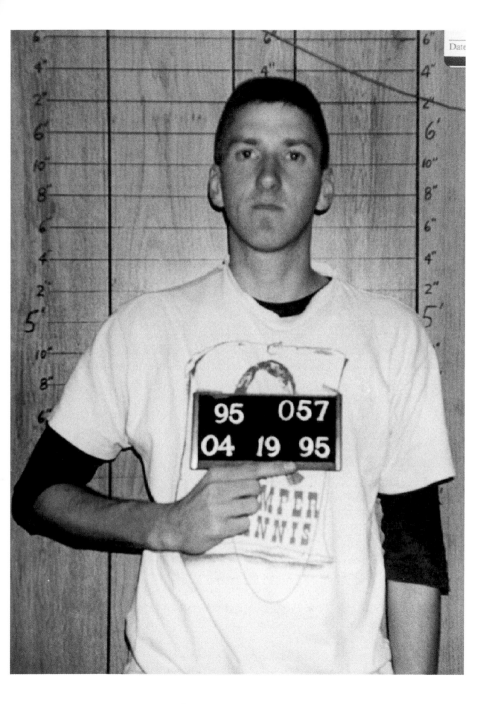

Oklahoma Bomber 479

The Bullet that Killed the Peace Process, 1995

One of the two bullets that killed Israeli Prime Minister Yitzhak Rabin.

Rabin, despite having a military background – serving with distinction during the Six Day War in 1967 – moved Israel closer to lasting peace with their Palestinian and Arab neighbours than any previous Israeli leader.

In 1993, his Labour government agreed to recognize the Palestinian Liberation Organization (PLO) as a legitimate political force and arranged for the incremental granting of limited self-rule to Palestinians in the Gaza Strip and the West Bank (also known as the Occupied Territories, as the Israelis hold them in defiance of a United Nations resolution). Rabin also agreed to stop new Israeli settlements being built in the Occupied Territories – the main way that previous Israeli governments had sought to consolidate their hold on the land covertly.

In 1994, Rabin and Shimon Peres, his foreign minister, shared the Nobel Peace Prize with PLO leader Yasir Arafat for their work towards a peace accord.

On 4 November 1995, Rabin was leaving a rally held in support of peace with the Palestinians when a 27-year-old Israeli right-wing student, Yigal Amir, stepped up to him and fired a pistol into his chest. Prime Minister Rabin died shortly afterwards in hospital.

Amir, who was sentenced to life for the murder, assassinated Rabin as a protest against the peace process. Subsequent Israeli prime ministers have been increasingly hawkish in comparison to Rabin.

The Unabomber, 1996

On 25 May 1978, a small parcel bomb mildly wounded a security guard at Illinois' Northwestern University. This was the first amateurish attack made by the serial killer who later became known as the Unabomber. Over the next 18 years, the Unabomber send home-made, but increasingly sophisticated parcel bombs to educational establishments and corporate businesses (he earned his name because he seemed to harbour a particular grudge against United Airlines). In all, the Unabomber injured 23 people, some severely, and killed three in 16 separate attacks.

In 1995, in the wake of the Oklahoma bombing, the Unabomber sent a "manifesto" to the *Washington Post* and the *New York Times* – threatening to blow up a passenger jet if it were not promptly published. It was a rambling and vitriolic screed that attacked big business, environmentally damaging government policies, academic and scientific research and progress in general. It was plain that the Unabomber believed that all development since the Industrial Revolution was dangerous, and he was willing to kill to make his point.

Fortunately, the manifesto was the last terrorist package the Unabomber was ever to send. David Kaczynski, in Montana, read the Unabomber's manifesto and realized with horror that it sounded just like the rantings of his hermit-like older brother Theodore. With natural misgivings, David informed the FBI, who raided Theodore's isolated Montana cabin and found plenty of proof that he was the Unabomber.

Theodore J. Kaczynski had been a brilliant academic, but in the late 1970s had apparently had an emotional breakdown and had become a virtual hermit – making bombs with some parts carefully hand-carved from wood, and rolling in hatred for the modern world. Ted Kaczynski was sentenced to four life sentences, with parole permanently denied.

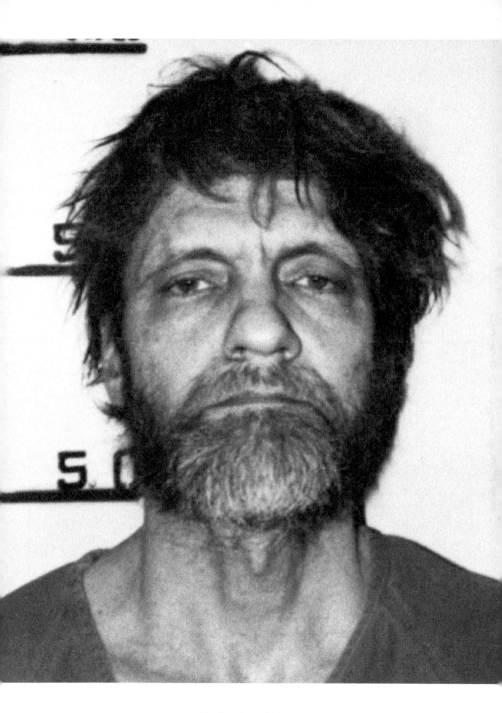

Unabomber 483

The Brussels Anti-Paedophile Demonstration, 1996

In 1996, the Belgian police arrested Marc Dutroux on a charge of kidnapping and child molestation. They had rescued two little girls from a house owned by Dutroux, but while he was being held for their kidnapping, two others, hidden in another of Dutroux's houses, died of starvation. The fact that investigating officers had searched this property while these two girls were still alive, yet failed to find their hidden cage or hear their cries, indicated a monumental blunder on behalf of the police. When their corpses were eventually found, the remains of two teenage girls were also discovered buried under the property.

Revelations of the Belgian police's stunning incompetence (and possibly corruption, as some suspected) over the Marc Dutroux child-murder case shocked the nation. On 20 October 1996, some 275,000 joined a march through Brussels protesting apparent police and government inactivity over paedophilia. Some even claimed that Dutroux was protected in his activities by a paedophile ring with members in the Belgian police, government and civil service.

The march was known as the White March, and among them the marchers carried this poster that reads: "The world is a dangerous place to live, not because of those who do evil, but because of those who look on and turn a blind eye."

" Le monde est dangereux
à vivre non à cause de
ceux qui font le mal mais
à cause de ceux qui
regardent et laissent faire."

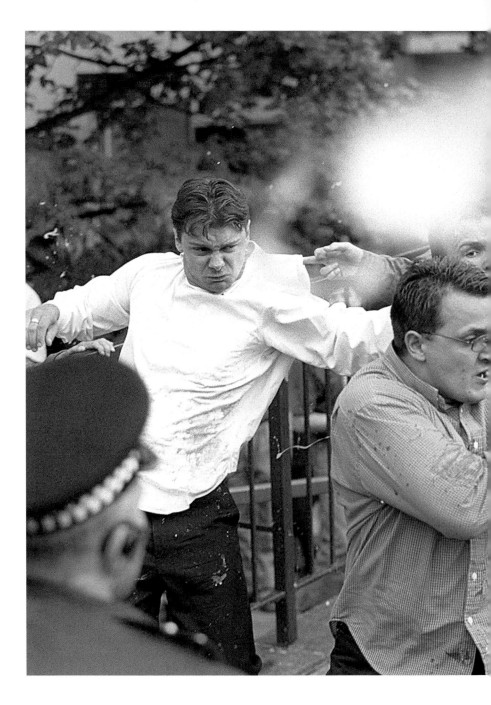

The Stephen Lawrence Murder, 1998

previous spread

The five white youths suspected of the racist murder of black teenager, Stephen Lawrence, in East London on 22 April 1993, are pelted with eggs by an angry crowd in 1998.

The brutality of the killing, the evidence of initial apathy and incompetence by investigators, and a subsequent report revealing that the London Metropolitan Police Division was riddled with "institutional racism" galvanized both indignation and strong feelings of anti-racism throughout Britain.

Unfortunately, despite much witness evidence that circumstantially linked the five to the killing, their trial was closed before the jury could reach a verdict. The key prosecution witness was declared "unreliable" by the trial judge, but it also cannot have helped that a tabloid newspaper had chosen to publish the names of the suspects before they could be bought up on charges. It was ruled that, under the circumstances, a fair trial was impossible.

Clinton's Denial, 1998

Speaking from the White House on 26 January 1999, Democrat President, William J. Clinton, categorically denies that he had had sexual contact with White House intern, Monica Lewinsky.

Later forced to testify on oath to the fact, however, Clinton equivocated and stretched word definitions to avoid being pinned down. At one point in his testimony, he responded to a question with the sentence: "It depends on what the meaning of the word 'is' is."

His reputation, both at home and abroad, suffered badly following this performance.

The Monica Lewinsky Affair, 1998

The infamous dress belonging to Monica Lewinsky. So keen was Special Prosecutor Kenneth Starr to prove that Lewinsky and President Bill Clinton had enjoyed sexual contact, he had semen stains on the dress DNA-finger-printed to prove that they belonged to Clinton.

The Republican-dominated House of Representatives impeached Clinton in December 1998, on charges of perjury and obstruction of justice. The Democrat-dominated Senate acquitted the president of all charges in 1999.

The Columbine High School Massacre, 1999

On 20 April 1999, students Dylan Klebold (right) and Eric Harris (left) walked into the cafeteria of the Columbine High School in Littleton, Colorado, and opened fire with semi-automatic handguns. Twelve students and a teacher died and over 30 other people were injured before the pair turned their guns on themselves.

The massacre at Columbine, and several similar incidents in the US, re-ignited the US debate on gun-control laws, but little has come of it since. Even the suggestion that children should not be allowed to carry weapons in school was attacked by vociferous elements of the pro-gun lobby.

I. 11:57:20 63 AM

Dr Harold Shipman, 2001

Manchester-based family doctor Harold Shipman was convicted on 31 January 2001 of murdering 15 of his elderly patients by injecting them with lethal doses of diamorphine (medical heroin).

Just why he did this is difficult to comprehend. Unlike most serial killers, there seems to have been no sexual or sadistic element to Shipman's murders: he killed most of his victims in their own homes, soothing them with a gentle bedside manner and, often, a cup of tea. Neither was there any financial motive – unlike killers like Henri Landru and Belle Gunness, Shipman made no effort to get potential victims to write him into their wills. Finally, these were definitely not mercy killings: although all his victims were elderly, few were seriously ill or even in particular discomfort.

As Shipman continues to deny that he ever harmed anybody, despite a mountain of evidence against him, we can only guess at why he killed. One possibly important fact may be that Shipman, at the age of 17, watched his own mother die of lung cancer. He would hurry home from college to comfort and chat with her, but it was only an injection of morphine, given by her doctor, that visibly eased her pain.

Was Shipman masochistically re-enacting his mother's own death each time he injected a lethal dose of diamorphine into an elderly patient? We may never know.

Some investigators believe that Shipman may have murdered as many as 265 of the 466 patients who died under his care as a family doctor in Rotherhide, Manchester. Unfortunately, as Shipman himself refuses to confess, and disinterment and effective forensic autopsies on so many bodies is practically impossible, we will probably never know just how many people Shipman murdered.

Harold Shipman   495

Slobodan Milosevic on Trial, 2001

Extradited Yugoslav leader, Slobodan Milosevic, faces The Hague War Crimes Tribunal, on charges of ethnic cleansing during the Yugoslavian civil war. At least 2,000 people were murdered and 400,000 were driven from their homes by Serb forces during the conflict (although this is an extremely conservative estimate). Few believe that these crimes could have taken place without Milosevic's knowledge and consent.

Milosevic adopted a combative stance before the court, labelling both his extradition and trial as illegal.

September 11th, 2001

On the morning of 11 September 2001, two hijacked Boeing 757 passenger jets were deliberately crashed into the New York World Trade Center (the first struck the North Tower at 8:45am, the second hit the South Tower at 9:06am). Both towers collapsed within an hour-and-a-half of the first impact. The death toll was 3,478 people.

At 9:40am, a third hijacked Boeing 757 struck the west side of the Pentagon building, Washington DC – the nerve-centre of the US Military – killing 190 people.

At 10:37am, the fourth and last hijacked plane crashed in open country-side near Shanksville Pennsylvania, killing all 45 on board. A mobile phone message from a passenger just before the crash said that he and some others were going to try to recapture the plane from the terrorists.

The hijackers were Islamic fundamentalists. The Al-Qaeda terrorist network, headed by the Saudi outlaw Osama bin Laden, is suspected of organizing the September 11th hijackings, though conclusive proof has yet to be offered in open court.

Index

Picture Acknowledgements

Getty Images
Slim Aarons 303; Nakram Al Akhbar 452-3; Arizona Historical Society Library 40-1; BWP Media 465; Ron Case 348-9; Tim Chapman 436-7; George Eastman House/Thomas Byrnes 43, William M Vander Weyde 63; Express Newspapers 51, 55, 57, 359, 369, 374-5, 386-7; Terry Fincher 421; Alexander Gardner 28-9; Greater Manchester Police 495; Bert Hardy 296-7; Shel Hershorn UT Austin 365; Shelly Katz 463; Joe Monroe 347; Museum of the City of New York/Jacob A Riis 65; National Archive 366-7; New York Times Co. 153; John Reardon/The Observer 459; Spencer Platt 499; Harold M Roberts/US Army 268-9; Santi Visalli Inc. 398-9; Sean Sexton 47; Will Waldron 471; Weegee 201, 209, 215, 219, 221, 223, 235, 237, 239, 240-1, 245, 259, 261, 263, 267

Press Association
473

Reuters
Reuters 479, 481, 425, 491; Vince Bucci 477; Gary Caskey 493; Grigory Dukor 461; Peter Dejong 497; Paul Hackett 486-7; Jasper Juinen 485; Wilfredo Lee 469; LAPD 475; Court Mast 457; Win McNamee 489; Pete Silva 456; Dick Yarwood 467

Robert Hunt Library
394-5

Topham Picturepoint
155, 281, 361, 363

All other images © Getty Images

Picture research: Ali Khoja

Special thanks to Elin Hagström and Liz Ihre in London and to Mitch Blank, Peter Rohowsky and Valerie Zars in New York